ASIA BOND MONITOR
MARCH 2020

ASIAN DEVELOPMENT BANK

ADB

ISBN 978-92-9262-152-0 (print), 978-92-9262-153-7 (electronic), 978-92-9262-154-4 (ebook)
ISSN 2219-1518 (print), 2219-1526 (electronic)
Publication Stock No. TCS200111-2
DOI: http://dx.doi.org/10.22617/TCS200111-2

The views expressed in this publication are those of the authors and do not necessarily reflect the views and policies of the Asian Development Bank (ADB) or its Board of Governors or the governments they represent.

ADB does not guarantee the accuracy of the data included in this publication and accepts no responsibility for any consequence of their use. The mention of specific companies or products of manufacturers does not imply that they are endorsed or recommended by ADB in preference to others of a similar nature that are not mentioned.

By making any designation of or reference to a particular territory or geographic area, or by using the term "country" in this document, ADB does not intend to make any judgments as to the legal or other status of any territory or area.

Corrigenda to ADB publications may be found at http://www.adb.org/publications/corrigenda.

Note:
ADB recognizes "Hong Kong", "Hongkong", and "Hong Kong Special Administrative Region" as Hong Kong, China; "China" as the People's Republic of China; "Korea" as the Republic of Korea; "Siam" as Thailand; "Vietnam" as Viet Nam; "Hanoi" as Ha Noi; and "Saigon" as Ho Chi Minh City.

Cover design by Erickson Mercado.

Contents

Emerging East Asian Local Currency Bond Markets: A Regional Update

Highlights

Key Trends

- Between 31 December 2019 and 29 February 2020, 2-year and 10-year local currency (LCY) government bond yields declined in major advanced economies, select European markets, and nearly all emerging East Asian markets amid heightened risk aversion due to the coronavirus disease 2019 (COVID-19) outbreak and an uncertain global economic growth outlook.[1]
- Many regional governments and central banks engaged in policy actions to mitigate the negative impact of COVID-19 on economic activities and financial markets. These include fiscal stimulus and monetary tools such as policy rate cuts and market operations.
- During the review period, regional equity markets all declined and credit default swap spreads widened on heightened negative investor sentiment driven by uncertainty related to COVID-19 and the economic outlook. All regional currencies weakened against the United States dollar, expect for the Japanese yen, as investors shifted their positions toward safe-haven assets.

- Foreign holdings' shares in the region's LCY government bond markets remained broadly stable in the fourth quarter of 2019. However, as the COVID-19 outbreak spread globally, risk-off sentiment resulted in some market sell-offs in January and February.
- Emerging East Asia's LCY bond market expanded to a size of USD16.0 trillion at the end of December, growing 12.5% year-on-year. Government bonds comprised 61.1% of the region's total LCY bonds outstanding.

Risks to Financial Stability

- The outbreak of COVID-19 remained the biggest source of uncertainty in the global economy and in financial markets.
- While trade tensions between the People's Republic of China and the United States abated with the signing of the Phase 1 trade deal, uncertainty over trade and globalization remain as long-term structural issues.
- Other downside risks include geopolitical issues associated with tensions in the Middle East that remained heightened.

---

[1] Emerging East Asia comprises the People's Republic of China; Hong Kong, China; Indonesia; the Republic of Korea; Malaysia; the Philippines; Singapore; Thailand; and Viet Nam.

Executive Summary

Global and Regional Market Developments

Government bond yields declined in major advanced economies, select European markets, and nearly all emerging East Asian markets between 31 December 2019 and 29 February 2020 due to a rise in risk-off sentiment amid the outbreak of the coronavirus disease 2019 (COVID-19) and uncertainty surrounding the global economic outlook.[1] To cushion the adverse impact of COVID-19 on economic activities and financial markets, a number of governments have utilized fiscal stimulus and/or monetary measures to support affected individuals and local businesses, and to stabilize financial markets.

As global investment sentiment soured, equity markets in the region posted losses, regional currencies weakened versus the United States (US) dollar, and credit default swap spreads widened. At the end of December 2019, the shares of foreign holdings in the region's LCY government bond markets were largely stable, but market sell-offs were observed in some markets in January and February due to heightened risk aversion.

Risks to the regional outlook remained tilted to the downside. The COVID-19 outbreak accounted for the biggest source of uncertainty in the global economy and financial markets. The absence of a long-term solution to the trade conflict between the People's Republic of China (PRC) and the US still challenges globalization and poses risks to the regional and global economy. Geopolitical issues relating to Middle East tensions also present uncertainty to the global economy and financial markets.

Bond Market Developments in Emerging East Asia

Emerging East Asia's local currency (LCY) bond market reached a size of USD16.0 trillion at the end of December, expanding 2.4% quarter-on-quarter (q-o-q) and 12.5% year-on-year (y-o-y).

Government bonds totaled USD9.8 trillion at the end of December on growth of 1.7% q-o-q and 11.4% y-o-y. Corporate bonds reached USD6.2 trillion, rising 3.5% q-o-q and 14.3% y-o-y. Government bonds accounted for 61.1% of the region's total LCY bond market, while corporate bonds comprised the remaining 38.9%.

The LCY bond market in the PRC accounted for 75.4% of emerging East Asia's total bonds outstanding at the end of December. The region's second-largest bond market was in the Republic of Korea, which accounted for 13.0% of total bonds outstanding. Markets in members of the Association of Southeast Asian Nations accounted for 9.8%.[2]

As a percentage of regional gross domestic product (GDP), emerging East Asia's LCY bond market was equivalent to 83.3% of regional GDP at the end of December, up from 82.6% at the end of September. The LCY bond markets of the Republic of Korea (130.5%) and Malaysia (104.6%) had the highest bonds outstanding-to-GDP ratios in the region.

LCY bond issuance in emerging East Asia totaled USD1,438.4 billion in the fourth quarter of 2019, falling 9.5% q-o-q but rising 12.5% y-o-y. Government bond issuance was USD715.7 billion, accounting for 49.8% of total issuance during the quarter, while corporate bond issuance was USD722.7 billion, accounting for 50.2% of total quarterly issuance.

---

[1] Emerging East Asia comprises the People's Republic of China; Hong Kong, China; Indonesia; the Republic of Korea; Malaysia; the Philippines; Singapore; Thailand; and Viet Nam.
[2] LCY bond statistics for the Association of Southeast Asian Nations include the markets of Indonesia, Malaysia, the Philippines, Singapore, Thailand, and Viet Nam.

The March issue of the *Asia Bond Monitor* includes four discussion boxes.

Box 1: The Economic Impact of COVID-19 on Developing Asia

This study assesses the effects of COVID-19 on economic activities in developing Asia.[3] Channels through which COVID-19 could affect economies include declines in domestic demand, reduced tourism and business travel, interruptions in trade and production linkages, supply disruptions, and negative health effects. The magnitude of the global economic impact will depend on how the outbreak evolves, which remains highly uncertain. The study explores a range of scenarios (best, moderate, and worst cases) and assesses the potential economic impact of each of these scenarios. COVID-19's global economic impact is expected to cost between USD76.7 billion and USD347.0 billion, or from 0.1% to 0.4% of global gross domestic product, with a midrange estimate of USD155.9 billion, or 0.2% of global gross domestic product. Two-thirds of the impact is expected to fall on the PRC. In developing Asia, most of the impact will be felt through reduced tourism. Some regional economies— such as Hong Kong, China; the Philippines; Singapore; and Viet Nam—will also be affected via trade and production linkages.

Box 2: How Are Financial Markets Reacting to the COVID-19 Outbreak?

This box reviews equity market reactions in three regional groupings as the outbreak of COVID-19 evolves: the PRC and Hong Kong, China; members of the Association of Southeast Asian Nations plus Japan and the Republic of Korea; and the rest of the world. The performances of sector-specific, capitalization-weighted indexes were tracked from 1 November 2019 to 29 February 2020 to reveal that (i) equity market reactions to COVID-19 shocks have largely occurred at the market-wide level; (ii) reactions were mild in response to outbreak-related

news in other markets and more pronounced in response to such news in local markets; and (iii) as more markets were affected across different regions, global equity markets experienced contagion in the form of a market slump during the last week of February.

Box 3: Green Bond Quantitative Performance during Periods of Market Stress—2020 Update

Box 3 presents a study by Nomura Asset Management, a Japanese asset management firm, on the quantitative performance of green bonds during periods of market stresses. The study explores whether green bonds demonstrate better risk-adjusted performance compared with conventional bonds. Using secondary market-pricing data, the study compared the performance of select EUR-denominated and USD-denominated green bonds against their conventional counterparts during periods of market stress. The results show that green bonds consistently outperformed their conventional equivalents during periods of market volatility and that the superior performance may be attributable to a green factor (after controlling for idiosyncratic variables). Moreover, the study finds evidence that the green factor may enhance an issuer's overall credit profile.

Box 4: The Alpha and Beta of ESG Investing

Box 4 presents the findings of Amundi, a European asset management firm, on the impact of environmental, social, and governance (ESG) factors on portfolio performance. The study showed that between 2014 and 2017 portfolios using ESG factors in select developed market equities outperformed. In particular, North American portfolios outperformed when using environmental factors, while European portfolios outperformed when using governance factors. An updated study in 2019 found that the alpha generated using ESG factors had declined in North America but was unchanged in the euro area.

---

[3] Developing Asia comprises the 46 developing member economies of the Asian Development Bank.

Global and Regional Market Developments

Bond yields fall in emerging East Asia amid an uncertain growth outlook and heightened risk aversion.

Between 31 December 2019 and 29 February 2020, 2-year and 10-year local currency government bond yields fell in all major advanced economies, a few select European markets, and most emerging East Asian economies on the back of risk-off investment sentiment fueled by the outbreak of the coronavirus disease 2019 (COVID-19) and an uncertain global economic growth outlook (**Table A**).[1]

In emerging East Asia, all 10-year government bond yields and nearly all 2-year government bond yields declined between 31 December and 29 February following a few policy rate cuts by central banks, heightened risk aversion due to the outbreak of COVID-19, and increased uncertainty in the regional economic outlook. Hong Kong, China saw the largest declines in 10-year and 2-year government bond yields at 77 and 51 basis points (bps), respectively. Several central banks in the region cut their policy rates during the review period and revised their economic growth forecast for 2020 downward (**Table B**). To mitigate the impact of COVID-19, the People's Bank

Table A: Changes in Global Financial Conditions

	2-Year Government Bond (bps)	10-Year Government Bond (bps)	5-Year Credit Default Swap Spread (bps)	Equity Index (%)	FX Rate (%)
Major Advanced Economies					
United States	(66)	(77)	–	(8.6)	–
United Kingdom	(24)	(38)	0.1	(12.8)	(3.3)
Japan	(12)	(14)	1	(10.7)	0.7
Germany	(17)	(42)	0.6	(10.3)	(1.7)
Emerging East Asia					
China, People's Rep. of	(40)	(41)	22	(5.6)	(0.4)
Hong Kong, China	(51)	(77)	–	(7.3)	(0.03)
Indonesia	(49)	(11)	39	(13.4)	(3.2)
Korea, Rep. of	(26)	(35)	14	(9.6)	(4.8)
Malaysia	(39)	(49)	28	(6.7)	(2.9)
Philippines	13	(15)	25	(13.1)	(0.6)
Singapore	(25)	(36)	–	(6.6)	(3.4)
Thailand	(36)	(42)	15	(15.1)	(5.8)
Viet Nam	20	(50)	20	(8.2)	(0.3)
Select European Markets					
Greece	3	(9)	60	(21.4)	(1.7)
Ireland	(9)	(31)	(0.1)	(10.9)	(1.7)
Italy	3	(26)	30	(6.5)	(1.7)
Portugal	4	(20)	10	(8.6)	(1.7)
Spain	(3)	(20)	7	(8.6)	(1.7)

( ) = negative, – = not available, bps = basis points, FX = foreign exchange.
Notes:
1. Data reflect changes between 31 December 2019 and 29 February 2020.
2. A positive (negative) value for the FX rate indicates the appreciation (depreciation) of the local currency against the United States dollar.
Sources: Bloomberg LP and Institute of International Finance.

---

[1] Emerging East Asia comprises the People's Republic of China; Hong Kong, China; Indonesia; the Republic of Korea; Malaysia; the Philippines; Singapore; Thailand; and Viet Nam.

Table B: Policy Rate Changes

Economies	Policy Rate 31-Dec-2019 (%)	Rate Changes		Policy Rate 29-Feb-2020 (%)	Year-to-Date Change in Policy Rates (basis points)
		Jan-2020 (%)	Feb-2020 (%)		
United States	1.75			1.75	
Euro Area	(0.50)			(0.50)	
Japan	(0.10)			(0.10)	
China, People's Rep. of	4.35			4.35	
Hong Kong, China	2.00			2.00	
Indonesia	5.00		↓ 0.25	4.75	↓ 25
Korea, Rep. of	1.25			1.25	
Malaysia	3.00	↓ 0.25		2.75	↓ 25
Philippines	4.00		↓ 0.25	3.75	↓ 25
Thailand	1.25		↓ 0.25	1.00	↓ 25
Viet Nam	6.00			6.00	

( ) = negative.
Note: Data as of 29 February 2019.
Source: Various central bank websites.

of China reduced banks' reserve requirement ratio by 50 bps on 6 January and cut an additional 10 bps from the medium-term lending facility rate on 16 February. Malaysia announced a 25-bps policy rate cut in January and another 25-bps reduction in March. The Bank of Thailand reduced the policy rate by 25 bps on 5 February and expects gross domestic product (GDP) growth to be slower than originally forecast due to the delayed passage of the budget and the impact of the coronavirus, among other reasons. This was followed by a 25-bps policy rate cut by the central bank in the Philippines on 6 February. Bank Indonesia lowered the 7-day reverse repurchase rate by 25 bps to 4.75% at its 19–20 February Board of Governors meeting. The Indonesian central bank also revised downward its 2020 economic growth forecast to 5.0%–5.4% from an earlier estimate of 5.1%–5.5%, reflecting the impact of the COVID-19 outbreak on the global economic recovery.

While the Monetary Authority of Singapore made no change to its monetary policy during the review period, the Government of Singapore passed its 2020 budget on 18 February that included fiscal stimulus to mitigate the negative economic impact of the COVID-19 outbreak in the short-term and bolster growth. These measures included a SGD5.6 billion special economic package and an SGD800 million increase in the Ministry of Health's budget. Singapore also downgraded its 2020 GDP forecast from between 0.5% and 2.5% to between -0.5% and 1.5% due to uncertainties regarding the impact of COVID-19. Similarly, the Bank of Korea lowered its 2020 GDP forecast to 2.0% from the 2.3% forecast announced in November. The government also announced a more than KRW20 trillion support package in response to

the COVID-19 outbreak. A supplemental budget worth KRW11.7 trillion is also being sought by the government. In Hong Kong, China, the government announced a broad stimulus package worth HKD120 billion, including cash handouts of HKD10,000 for residents aged 18 years old and above.

However, the continued spread of COVID-19 and the economic impact of quarantine measures led to a number of central banks easing in March. On 16 March, the Bank of Korea conducted an emergency policy rate cut of 50 bps. The State Bank of Vietnam also announced a 100-bps cut on its refinancing rate effective 17 March. On 19 March, the Bangko Sentral ng Pilipinas followed with a 50-bps policy rate cut while Bank Indonesia announced a 25-bps reduction to its policy rate.

Monetary stances in major advanced economies remained stable during the observation period (Table B). The United States (US) Federal Reserve left the federal funds rate unchanged at between 1.50% and 1.75% during its 28–29 January monetary policy meeting, noting that the US economy continued to post gains as the labor market remained robust. The Federal Reserve also highlighted its concern over lower-than-targeted inflation in 2019. Personal Consumption Expenditures inflation in the US rose slightly to 1.7% in January from 1.5% in December, which was still below the targeted rate of 2.0%. US GDP expanded 2.1% year-on-year (y-o-y) in the fourth quarter of 2019, the same as in the previous quarter. December GDP growth forecasts remained unchanged from prior forecasts in September at 2.0% for 2020, 1.9% for 2021, and 1.8% for 2022. The US labor market remained strong, with January nonfarm payrolls rising to 273,000 from 184,000 in December and the unemployment rate holding steady at 3.6% in January. As COVID-19 spread to more economies around the world, global stock markets slumped significantly since late February and continued to fall further in March. The evolving impact of COVID-19 led to an intensification of policy actions, with the Federal Reserve implementing an emergency rate cut of 50 bps on 3 March. This was followed soon after by an additional 100 bps rate cut on 15 March and additional asset purchases.

The European Central Bank (ECB) left monetary policy unchanged on 23 January, with the interest rates on main refinancing operations, the marginal lending facility, and the deposit facility held at 0.00%, 0.25%, and −0.50%, respectively. The monthly purchase amount of EUR20 billion under the asset purchase program was also left unchanged. The ECB noted moderate economic growth, with euro area GDP expanding 0.9% y-o-y in the fourth quarter of 2019, down from 1.2% y-o-y in the previous quarter. The 2020 GDP growth forecast was slightly downgraded to 1.1% in December from 1.2% in September, while growth forecasts for 2021 and 2022 were left unchanged at 1.4% each. As the COVID-19 continues to evolve to more European markets, ECB announced on 2 March that it was closely monitoring the situation and stood ready to respond if needed. On 12 March, the ECB announced further measures, with an additional annual asset purchase of EUR120 billion. The forecast for GDP in 2020 was also lowered to 0.8% and 1.3% for 2021. On 19 March, the ECB responded even more strongly and launched a EUR750 billion Pandemic Asset Purchase Programme.

In January, the Bank of Japan (BOJ) left unchanged its monetary policy rate at −0.1%, the 10-year government bond yield at 0.0%, and the asset purchase program at JPY80 trillion per year for Japan Government Bonds. Following the passage of spending measures by the Government of Japan, the fiscal year 2019 GDP growth estimate was raised to 0.8% in January from October's estimate of 0.6%, while GDP growth forecasts for 2020 and 2021 were raised to 0.9% and 1.1%, respectively, from 0.7% and 1.0%. To mitigate the negative impact of COVID-19 on economic activities in 2020, the BOJ injected JPY500 billion in financial markets via reverse repurchase agreements on 2 March. On 16 March, the BOJ engaged in additional easing measures, doubling its asset purchases of exchange-traded funds.

Economic Outlook

Global growth had been widely expected to strengthen in 2020 and 2021 relative to 2019, but this assessment is being challenged by a major new source of uncertainty. According to the International Monetary Fund's (IMF) *World Economic Outlook Update January 2020*, the global economy grew an estimated 2.9% in 2019 and is projected to expand 3.3% in 2020 and 3.4% in 2021. However, these projections were made prior to the COVID-19 outbreak.

Even before the onset of COVID-19, economic forecasts were being downgraded due to negative shocks in India and other emerging markets. The IMF lowered its global growth projections by 0.1 percentage points for 2020 and 0.2 percentage points for 2021 compared with its October 2019 projections. World trade is expected to expand 2.9% in 2020 and 3.7% in 2021, up from 1.0% in 2019. Trade tensions between the People's Republic of China (PRC) and the US continued to pose a major downside risk to global growth prospects. On 15 January, the world's two biggest economies signed a Phase 1 trade deal under which the US agreed to cut some tariffs on imports from the PRC in exchange for PRC commitments to buy more US farm, energy, and manufactured products. However, the deal is temporary and limited in scope, and falls far short of a comprehensive settlement. Geopolitical tensions in the Middle East pose another downside risk. On a positive note, global financial conditions remain broadly benign and monetary policy stances are largely accommodative.

The IMF's projections of stronger global growth are largely predicated on assumptions of stronger growth in emerging markets and developing economies, which will outweigh the downward growth trajectory of advanced economies. The US economy is expected to grow 2.0% in 2020 and 1.7% in 2021, down from 2.3% in 2019. The advanced economies as a whole are forecast to expand 1.6% in both 2020 and 2021, slightly down from 1.7% in 2019. On the other hand, growth in emerging markets and developing economies is projected to increase to 4.4% in 2020 and 4.6% in 2021 from 3.7% in 2019.

The IMF projects consumer price inflation in emerging markets and developing economies to fall from 5.1% in 2019 to 4.6% in 2020 and 4.5% in 2021. The corresponding figures for advanced economies are 1.4%, 1.7%, and 1.9%. Weak global oil prices are limiting inflationary pressures around the world.

COVID-19 poses a major downside risk to global growth but it will have the biggest negative economic impact on developing Asia.[2] The disease first erupted in the PRC, which is expected to suffer the bulk of the economic fallout from the outbreak. Given its outsized effect on other Asian economies, the negative impact of the disease on the PRC will inevitably spill over to the rest of the region, most notably East and Southeast Asian economies with extensive trade and other linkages with the PRC.

The Asian Development Bank's (ADB) *Asian Development Outlook 2019 Supplement*, released in December, forecast the region's economy to expand 5.2% in 2020 after growing 5.9% in 2018 and an estimated 5.2% in 2019. The PRC, which grew 6.6% in 2018 and an estimated 6.1% in 2019, is projected to expand 5.8%. The 2018, 2019, and 2020 figures for the 10 members of the Association of Southeast Asian Nations are 5.0%, 4.4%, and 4.7%, respectively. GDP in the Republic of Korea is projected to grow 2.3% in 2020 after rising 2.7% in 2018 and an estimated 2.0% in 2019. The growth figures for Hong Kong, China are 3.0% in 2018, an estimated –1.2% in 2019, and a projected 0.3% in 2020. The ADB report notes that the region faces a challenging external environment, in particular persistent trade tensions between the PRC and the US, which adversely affects not only exports but also business sentiment and investment. According to the ADB report, the region's consumer price inflation will increase from 2.4% in 2018 to an estimated 2.8% in 2019 and further to 3.1% in 2020.

COVID-19 has emerged as a major source of uncertainty for the global and regional economic outlook, as explained in **Box 1**. The accuracy of the economic outlook discussed above will depend heavily on the evolution of the disease. If it is contained relatively quickly, there is much greater cause for optimism about the economic outlook for Asia and the world. If, on the other hand, the disease persists for an extended period, the economic damage is bound to be more substantial. Current estimates of the negative impact of COVID-19 on the PRC's GDP growth in 2020 typically range from 0.3% to 1.7%. The corresponding figures for the rest of developing Asia range from 0.2% to 0.5%. In summary, all growth projections are subject to a great deal of uncertainty due to COVID-19.

The outbreak and evolution of COVID-19, as well as its impact on the global economic outlook, has significantly affected risk sentiment in financial markets even if the economic impact will likely be confined to a short-term horizon. Between 31 December 2019 and 29 February 2020, all regional equity markets fell on the back of moderating global growth and heightened risk aversion driven by COVID-19 (**Figure A**). Emerging East Asian currencies also depreciated during the review period on a weaker global growth outlook (**Figure B**). Heightened risk aversion and associated economic growth moderation pushed up credit default swap spreads, the CBOE Volatility Index, and JP Morgan Emerging Markets Bond Index Sovereign Stripped Spreads (**Figures C**, **D**, and **E**).

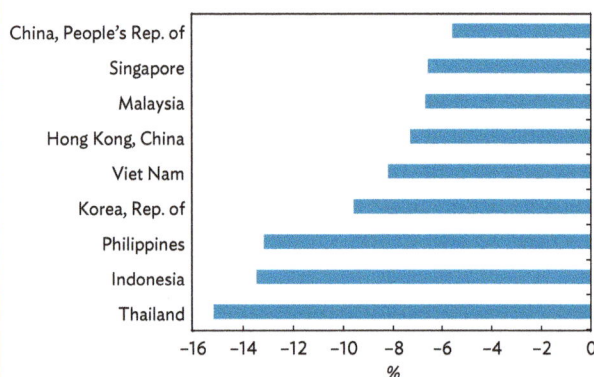

Figure A: Changes in Equity Indexes in Emerging East Asia

Note: Changes between 31 December 2019 and 29 February 2020.
Source: Bloomberg LP.

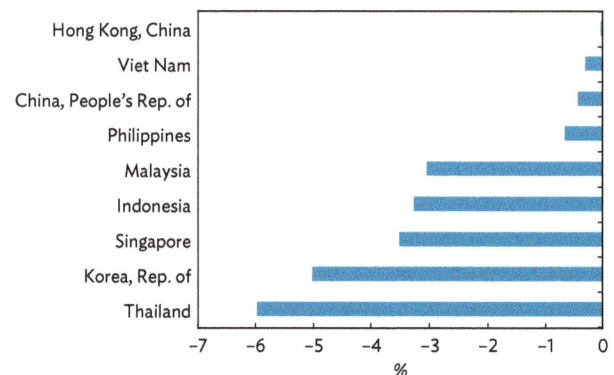

Figure B: Changes in Month-End Spot Exchange Rates vs. the United States Dollar

Notes:
1. Changes between 31 December 2019 and 29 February 2020.
2. A positive (negative) value for the foreign exchange rate indicates the appreciation (depreciation) of the local currency against the United States dollar.
Source: Bloomberg LP.

---

[2]   Developing Asia comprises the 46 developing member economies of the Asian Development Bank.

Figure C: Credit Default Swap Spreads in Select Asian Markets (senior 5-year)

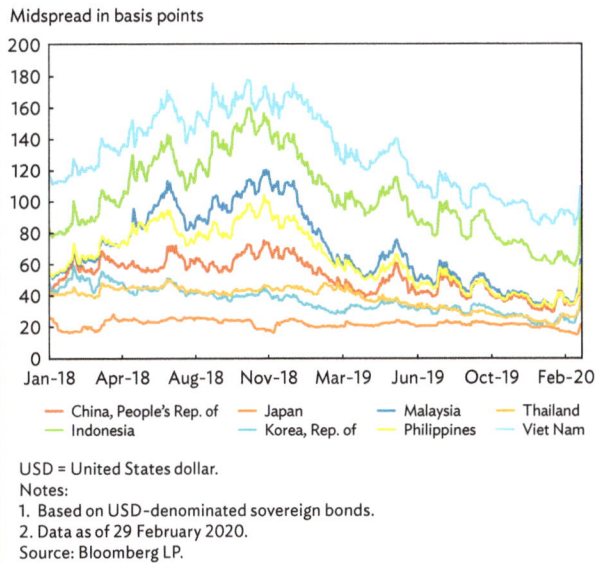

Midspread in basis points

Legend: China, People's Rep. of; Japan; Malaysia; Thailand; Indonesia; Korea, Rep. of; Philippines; Viet Nam

USD = United States dollar.
Notes:
1. Based on USD-denominated sovereign bonds.
2. Data as of 29 February 2020.
Source: Bloomberg LP.

Figure D: United States Equity Volatility and Emerging Market Sovereign Bond Spread

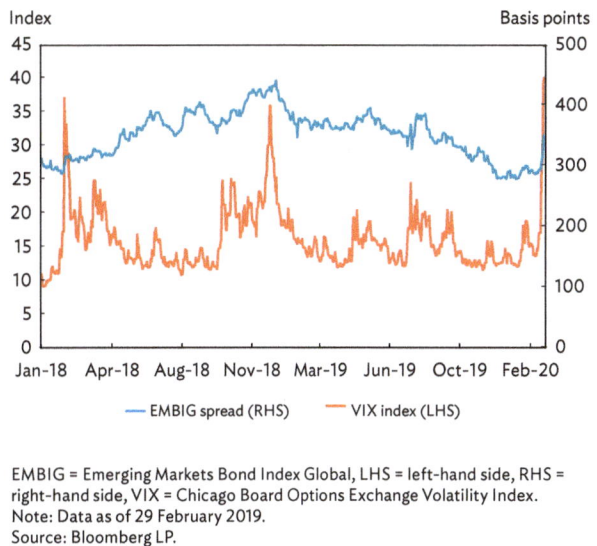

Index / Basis points

Legend: EMBIG spread (RHS); VIX index (LHS)

EMBIG = Emerging Markets Bond Index Global, LHS = left-hand side, RHS = right-hand side, VIX = Chicago Board Options Exchange Volatility Index.
Note: Data as of 29 February 2019.
Source: Bloomberg LP.

To further understand equity markets' reaction to the outbreak of COVID-19, **Box 2** examines the sectoral performance of stocks in the PRC and Hong Kong, China; other emerging East Asian markets; and markets other than emerging East Asia. Different sectors have largely reacted to COVID-19 at the market level and the stock market's reaction to the outbreak is more pronounced in economies once cases start to rapidly increase. Global stock markets also showed contagion during the market slump in the last week of February.

Foreign holdings of local currency government bonds in emerging East Asia were largely stable during the review period (**Figure F**). The largest gains in the foreign holdings' share occurred in Malaysia, following portfolio rebalancing activities. Foreign holdings also increased in the PRC as investors continued to invest in the bond market.

Risks to Emerging East Asian Bond Markets

Overall, downside risks continue to outweigh upside risks. Prior to the outbreak of COVID-19, there was a growing consensus that although risks were tilted to the downside, the gap between upside and downside risks was declining. However, the outbreak of COVID-19, which is by far the biggest downside risk to emerging East Asia's economic outlook and financial stability, has significantly rewidened the gap. In fact, the disease

Figure E: JP Morgan Emerging Markets Bond Index Sovereign Stripped Spreads

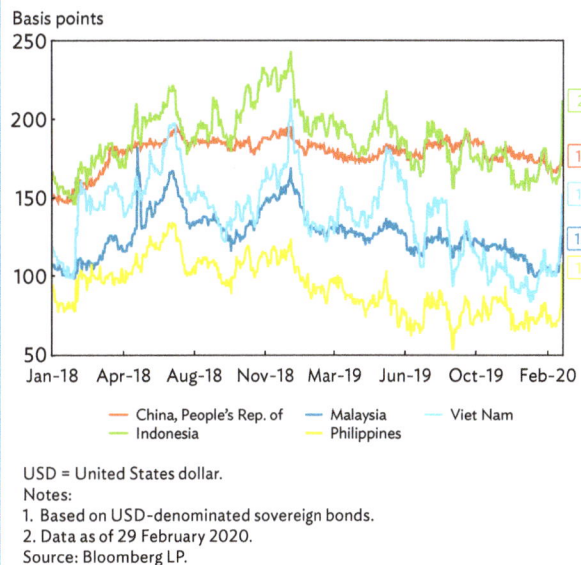

Basis points

Values: 211, 178, 152, 130, 108

Legend: China, People's Rep. of; Malaysia; Viet Nam; Indonesia; Philippines

USD = United States dollar.
Notes:
1. Based on USD-denominated sovereign bonds.
2. Data as of 29 February 2020.
Source: Bloomberg LP.

has overtaken the PRC–US trade conflict as the single biggest source of uncertainty surrounding the world economy and global financial markets.

COVID-19 first emerged in Wuhan, a large city of more than 10 million in Hubei province in the central PRC, in December 2019. The number of infections and fatalities spread like wildfire across much of the PRC

Box 1: The Economic Impact of COVID-19 on Developing Asia

The coronavirus disease 2019 (COVID-19) was first identified in the city of Wuhan in the People's Republic of China (PRC) in December 2019.[a] The number of confirmed cases has grown rapidly since then, spreading initially in the PRC and subsequently in the Republic of Korea, Italy, Iran, and other economies. At the end of February 2020, COVID-19 had infected 85,403 people in 55 economies and caused 2,924 deaths worldwide. The number of cases and fatalities from COVID-19 has already far surpassed the corresponding figures for the severe acute respiratory syndrome (SARS) outbreak in 2003. While COVID-19 is first and foremost a public health crisis, it is bound to have sizable economic repercussions, an issue we explore in this box.

Channels of Economic Impact

There are several channels through which COVID-19 can affect economic activity. These include a decline in domestic consumption and possibly investment, a decline in tourism and business travel, spillovers from weakened demand into other sectors and economies through trade and production linkages, supply-side disruptions to production and trade, and effects on public health and health care spending.

Domestic consumption in the PRC is experiencing a temporary but sharp decline due to behavioral and policy changes as people stay home either as a precaution or because they have been told to. This also occurred during the SARS outbreak in 2003, when retail sales in the PRC declined by almost 3 percentage points during the second quarter of 2003 (**Figure B1.1**). The magnitude of the consumption shock during the current outbreak could well be bigger than in 2003 depending on the length and severity of the outbreak, as well as the policy responses. In the scenario of a protracted outbreak that affects companies' long-term business plans, a decline in investment is also possible.

Other developing Asian economies outside of the PRC will be affected through tourism and business travel.[b] Tourism is an important source of revenue for many economies in the region, and visitors from the PRC account for a large and growing share of tourists throughout developing Asia (**Figure B1.2**). Tourism arrivals and receipts are expected to decline sharply as a result of travel bans and precautionary behavior. Many airlines have suspended or severely curtailed flights to the PRC. Non-Chinese tourist arrivals are also expected to decline as tourists avoid traveling in the region. During the SARS outbreak, Southeast and East Asian countries—such as Indonesia, Thailand, and the

Figure B1.1: Retail Sales and Personal Consumption Expenditures in the People's Republic of China during the SARS Outbreak, 2002–2003 (y-o-y, %)

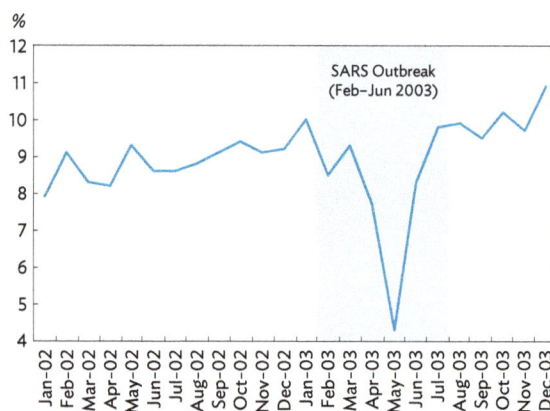

SARS = severe acute respiratory syndrome.
Note: From Asian Development Bank. 2020. *The Economic Impact of the COVID-19 Outbreak on Developing Asia.* https://www.adb.org/publications/economic-impact-covid19-developing-asia.
Sources: Haver Analytics, CEIC Data Company, World Health Organization, and Asian Development Bank.

Republic of Korea—witnessed declines in tourist arrivals from outside Asia even though they had very few SARS cases (**Figure B1.3**).

Demand shocks can spill over into other sectors and economies via trade and production linkages. The PRC is a major export market for many developing Asian economies (**Figure B1.4**). As such, a sharp drop in the PRC's demand for goods and services is likely to be felt across the region.

Supply-side disruptions will also reverberate across the region and the world. The PRC is at the center of global manufacturing value chains. Many economies export large amounts of intermediate goods to the PRC and use inputs from the PRC in their production processes. COVID-19 has seriously disrupted production in the PRC due to business closures and the inability of workers to move freely between home and work. These disruptions will negatively impact production in and trade with other economies, especially those in East and Southeast Asia that are closely intertwined with the PRC in regional production networks.

Finally, COVID-19 may also entail long-term health effects via mortality and morbidity, and through an increase in (and diversion of) health care expenditures.

---

[a] This box is a shortened version of Asian Development Bank. 2020. *The Economic Impact of the COVID-19 Outbreak on Developing Asia.* https://www.adb.org/publications/economic-impact-covid19-developing-asia.
[b] Developing Asia comprises the 46 developing member economies of the Asian Development Bank.

continued on next page

Box 1: The Economic Impact of COVID-19 on Developing Asia   *continued*

Figure B1.2: Tourist Arrivals from the People's Republic of China as a Share of Total Arrivals, 2018

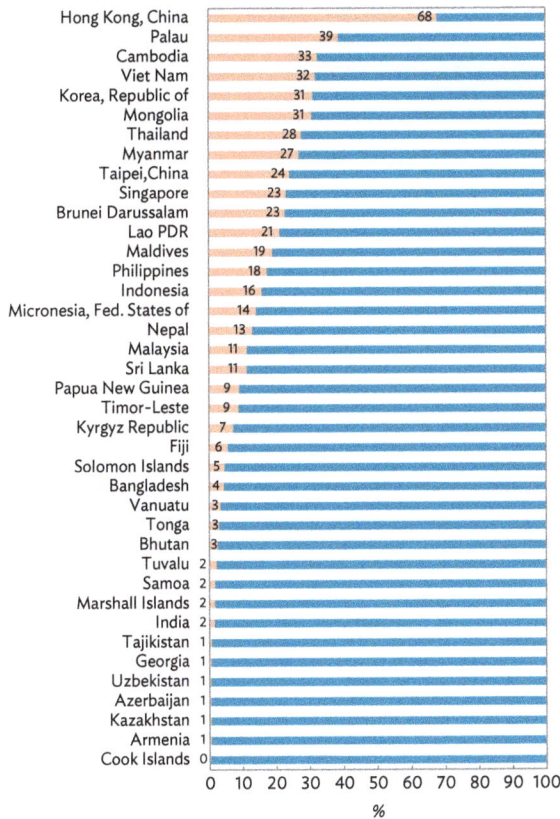

Economy	%
Hong Kong, China	68
Palau	39
Cambodia	33
Viet Nam	32
Korea, Republic of	31
Mongolia	31
Thailand	28
Myanmar	27
Taipei,China	24
Singapore	23
Brunei Darussalam	23
Lao PDR	21
Maldives	19
Philippines	18
Indonesia	16
Micronesia, Fed. States of	14
Nepal	13
Malaysia	11
Sri Lanka	11
Papua New Guinea	9
Timor-Leste	9
Kyrgyz Republic	7
Fiji	6
Solomon Islands	5
Bangladesh	4
Vanuatu	3
Tonga	3
Bhutan	3
Tuvalu	2
Samoa	2
Marshall Islands	2
India	2
Tajikistan	1
Georgia	1
Uzbekistan	1
Azerbaijan	1
Kazakhstan	1
Armenia	1
Cook Islands	0

Lao PDR = Lao People's Democratic Republic.
Source: World Tourism Organization.

Figure B1.3: Tourist Arrivals from Outside Asia to Select Developing Member Economies, 2002–2004

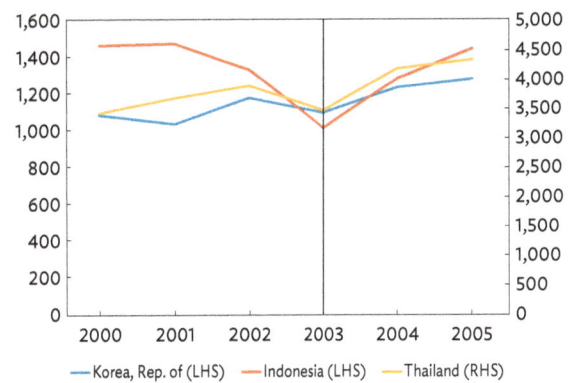

LHS = left-hand side, RHS = right-hand side.
Source: World Tourism Organization.

Figure B1.4: Exports to the People's Republic of China by Percentage of Gross Domestic Product, 2016–2018 Average

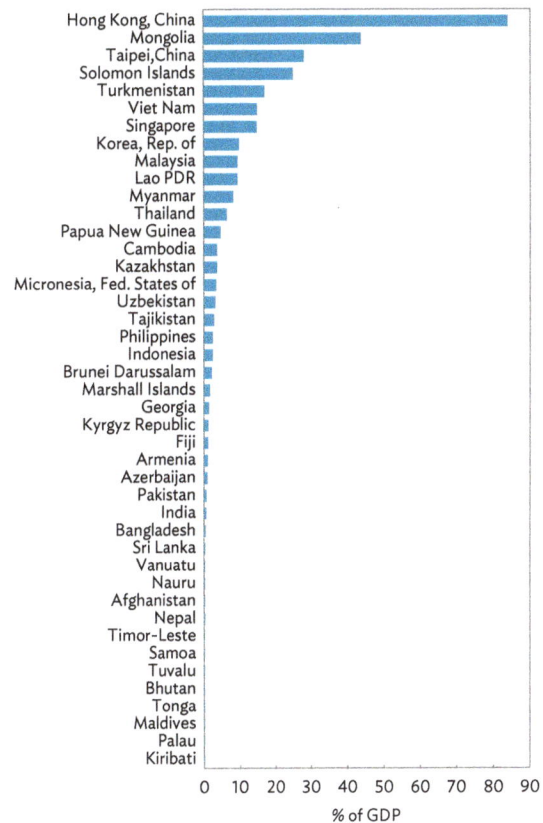

Economies in order: Hong Kong, China; Mongolia; Taipei,China; Solomon Islands; Turkmenistan; Viet Nam; Singapore; Korea, Rep. of; Malaysia; Lao PDR; Myanmar; Thailand; Papua New Guinea; Cambodia; Kazakhstan; Micronesia, Fed. States of; Uzbekistan; Tajikistan; Philippines; Indonesia; Brunei Darussalam; Marshall Islands; Georgia; Kyrgyz Republic; Fiji; Armenia; Azerbaijan; Pakistan; India; Bangladesh; Sri Lanka; Vanuatu; Nauru; Afghanistan; Nepal; Timor-Leste; Samoa; Tuvalu; Bhutan; Tonga; Maldives; Palau; Kiribati.

Lao PDR = Lao People's Democratic Republic.
Source: CEIC Data Company (accessed 10 February 2020).

Estimated Economic Impacts under Several Scenarios

The magnitude of the economic impact of COVID-19 will depend on the outbreak's evolution, which continues to be very unpredictable. Any analysis of COVID-19's impact thus requires experimenting with multiple scenarios. The Asian Development Bank (ADB) explored four scenarios with detailed assumptions that are explained in **Table B1.1**. As COVID-19 evolves, ADB will regularly update its assessment, with the next update to be included in the *Asian Development Outlook 2020*, which will be launched on 1 April.

The multiscenario analysis suggests a global impact in the range of USD77 billion–USD347 billion, or 0.1%–0.4% of global gross domestic product (GDP), with a moderate case estimate of USD156 billion, or 0.2% of global GDP (**Table B1.2**). Two-thirds of the impact will fall on the PRC,

continued on next page

Box 1: The Economic Impact of COVID-19 on Developing Asia   *continued*

Table B1.1: Full Set of Scenario Assumptions

Scenario	Channel / Duration of Travel Bans and Sharp Decline in Domestic Demand	Tourism and Travel Bans	Decline in PRC Consumption Relative to No-Outbreak Scenario	Decline in PRC Investment Relative to No-Outbreak Scenario	Decline in Domestic Consumption in Selected Economy
Best case	2 months	- Chinese outbound tourism drops by 50% for 2 months. - For economies imposing travel bans, no tourism receipts from the PRC for 2 months. - Inbound PRC tourism and receipts fall by as much as during the SARS outbreak. - Tourism from outside Asia to non-PRC East and Southeast Asian economies falls by as much as during the SARS outbreak (assume peak decline lasts 2 months).	0.7% (based on 2.75-pp decline in retail sales growth in Q32003 vs. prior 9 quarters)	None	None
Moderate case	3 months	- Chinese outbound tourism drops by 50% for 3 months. - For economies imposing travel bans, no tourism receipts from the PRC for 3 months. - Inbound PRC tourism and receipts fall by an additional 10% relative to the base case. - Tourism from outside Asia to non-PRC East and Southeast Asian economies falls by an additional 10% relative to the best case (i.e., 1 additional month).	2% (based on 2-pp decline in PCE growth in 2003 vs. 2000–2002 average)	None	None
Worst case	6 months	- Chinese outbound tourism drops by 50% for 6 months. - For economies imposing travel bans, no tourism receipts from the PRC for 6 months. - Inbound PRC tourism and receipts fall by an additional 30% relative to the base case. - Tourism from outside Asia to non-PRC East and Southeast Asian economies falls by an additional 40% relative to the best case (i.e., 4 additional months).	2% (based on 2-pp decline in PCE growth in 2003 vs. 2000–2002 average)	2% (protracted outbreak worsens business sentiment)	None
Hypothetical worst case (specific to each selected economy)	6 months; plus outbreak in selected economy lasting 3 months	- Chinese outbound tourism drops by 50% for 6 months - For economies imposing travel bans, no tourism receipts from the PRC for 6 months. - Inbound PRC tourism and receipts fall by an additional 30% relative to the base case. - Tourism from outside Asia to non-PRC East and Southeast Asian economies falls by an additional 40% relative to the best case (i.e., 4 additional months).	2% (based on 2-pp decline in PCE growth in 2003 vs. 2000–2002 average)	2% (protracted outbreak worsens business sentiment)	2% (selected economy only)

DMC = developing member country, PCE = personal consumption expenditure, pp = percentage point, PRC = People's Republic of China, SARS = severe acute respiratory syndrome.
Source: Asian Development Bank. 2020. *The Economic Impact of the COVID-19 Outbreak on Developing Asia.* https://www.adb.org/publications/economic-impact-covid19-developing-asia.

Table B1.2: Estimated Global and Regional Impact of COVID-19 under Different Scenarios

	Best Case		Moderate Case		Worst Case	
	% of GDP	Losses (USD million)	% of GDP	Losses (USD million)	% of GDP	Losses (USD million)
World	−0.089	76,693	−0.182	155,948	−0.404	346,975
People's Republic of China	−0.323	43,890	−0.757	103,056	−1.740	236,793
Developing Asia (excluding the People's Republic of China)	−0.171	15,658	−0.244	22,284	−0.463	42,243
Rest of the World	−0.011	17,145	−0.020	30,608	−0.044	67,938

GDP = gross domestic product, USD = United States dollar.
Source: Asian Development Bank. 2020. *The Economic Impact of the COVID-19 Outbreak on Developing Asia.* https://www.adb.org/publications/economic-impact-covid19-developing-asia.

where the outbreak has been concentrated so far. In the moderate scenario, the economic loss to the PRC relative to a no-outbreak scenario is USD103 billion, or nearly 0.8% of domestic GDP. The remainder of the impact on the global economy is split roughly equally between the rest of developing Asia and the rest of the world. Specifically, the

rest of developing Asia would suffer a loss of USD22 billion, or 0.2% of its GDP, under the moderate scenario.

The main channel through which many economies in developing Asia will be affected is through a substantial drop in tourism demand (**Table B1.3**). There is anecdotal evidence

continued on next page

Box 1: The Economic Impact of COVID-19 on Developing Asia   *continued*

Table B1.3: Decline in Tourism Revenues in Emerging East Asia

	Best Case		Moderate Case		Worst Case	
	% of GDP	Losses (USD million)	% of GDP	Losses (USD million)	% of GDP	Losses (USD million)
Cambodia	−1.409	−345.7	−1.929	−473.4	−3.490	−856.5
Hong Kong, China	−0.906	−3,286.7	−1.178	−4,273.6	−1.995	−7,234.1
Thailand	−0.845	−4,265.8	−1.224	−6,180.2	−2.361	−11,923.5
Singapore	−0.739	−2,692.8	−0.941	−3,427.4	−1.546	−5,631.3
Viet Nam	−0.432	−1,059.2	−0.614	−1,504.6	−1.158	−2,840.6
Philippines	−0.242	−801.4	−0.352	−1,164.4	−0.681	−2,253.6
Indonesia	−0.166	−1,730.5	−0.207	−2,155.9	−0.329	−3,432.1
Lao People's Democratic Republic	−0.164	−29.5	−0.231	−41.5	−0.431	−77.4
Malaysia	−0.163	−584.3	−0.212	−762.0	−0.361	−1,295.0
Myanmar	−0.149	−106.3	−0.224	−159.4	−0.448	−318.8
China, People's Rep. of	−0.112	−15,241.6	−0.149	−20,215.0	−0.258	−35,135.3
Brunei Darussalam	−0.086	−11.7	−0.113	−15.3	−0.192	−26.1
Korea, Rep. of	−0.073	−1,184.5	−0.103	−1,671.7	−0.193	−3,133.3

GDP = gross domestic product, USD = United States dollar.
Source: Asian Development Bank. 2020. *The Economic Impact of the COVID-19 Outbreak on Developing Asia.* https://www.adb.org/publications/economic-impact-covid19-developing-asia.

that tourism arrivals in many developing Asian economies dropped between 50% and 90% in February relative to the prior year. Overall estimates suggest a loss of USD15 billion–USD35 billion in tourism receipts for the PRC and USD19 billion–USD45 billion for the rest of developing Asia.

Developing Asian economies with strong trade and production linkages with the PRC—such as Hong Kong, China; Singapore; Viet Nam; and the Philippines—will also be materially affected by the COVID-19 outbreak. For many economies in the region, the PRC is both a significant source of foreign tourists and a major export destination (Figure B1.4).

The estimated impact on individual economies—and sectors—could be much larger under a hypothetical worst-case scenario in which a given economy experiences a significant outbreak of its own (**Figure B1.5**). The epidemiological evolution of COVID-19, which will significantly affect its economic impact, remains highly fluid. The disease has begun to spread more forcefully outside of the PRC, with the Republic of Korea, Iran, and Italy witnessing large outbreaks. In addition, global equity markets and oil prices suffered huge losses in the first 2 weeks of March. As mentioned above, ADB will continue to monitor new developments and update its assessment, which will be included in *Asian Development Outlook 2020* to be released on 1 April.

Figure B1.5: Global Value Chain Exposure to the People's Republic of China for Select Economies, 2018

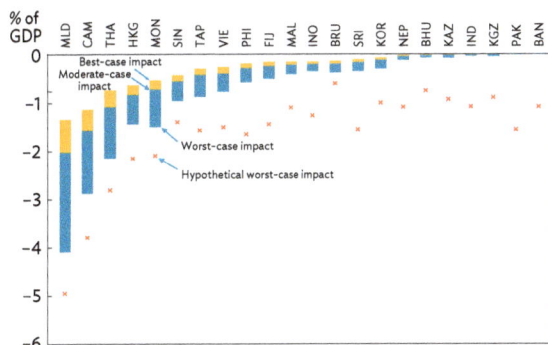

BAN = Bangladesh; BHU = Bhutan; BRU = Brunei Darussalam; CAM = Cambodia; FIJ = Fiji; HKG = Hong Kong, China; IND = India; INO = Indonesia; KAZ = Kazakhstan; KGZ = Kyrgyz Republic; KOR = Republic of Korea; LAO = Lao People's Democratic Republic; MAL = Malaysia; MLD = Maldives; MON = Mongolia; NEP = Nepal; PAK = Pakistan; PHI = Philippines; SIN = Singapore; SRI = Sri Lanka; TAP = Taipei,China; THA = Thailand; VIE = Viet Nam.
Notes: Bars indicate the range of estimated impact, with the top of the bar indicating the best-case scenario impact, the midline indicating the moderate scenario impact, and the bottom of the bar indicating the worst-case scenario impact. The marker shows the economic impact of a hypothetical worst-case scenario where a significant outbreak occurs in that economy. These should not be interpreted as a prediction that an outbreak will occur in any of these economies; in most of these economies there are very few cases of COVID-19. Rather, they are meant to guide policy makers in determining how costly an outbreak could be so they can properly evaluate the benefits and costs of prevention and early response.
Source: Asian Development Bank estimates.

Box 2: How Are Financial Markets Reacting to the COVID-19 Outbreak?

The recent outbreak of the coronavirus disease 2019 (COVID-19) in the People's Republic of China (PRC) had infected more than 85,000 people and caused more than 2,900 deaths as of 29 February 2020.[a] To fight against the spread of the virus, the Government of the PRC mobilized vast resources and restricted many normal economic activities. These developments will weigh on economic growth in the first quarter of 2020 and beyond. While COVID-19's impact on the real economy will eventually be revealed in actual economic performance indicators, the ongoing reaction of equity markets can serve as a forward-looking signal of the potential economic impacts.

To understand how global equity markets are reacting to the spread of COVID-19, we develop sector-specific, capitalization-weighted indexes of stocks in different regions and observe the movements of these indexes. To observe the patterns of equity market reactions in different regions, listed stocks are classified into one of three regions: (i) the PRC and Hong Kong, China; (ii) the Association of Southeast Asian Nations (ASEAN) plus the Republic of Korea and Japan (collectively known as ASEAN+2); and (iii) the rest of the world.[a] For each regional pool, the stocks are further grouped into sectors based on Bloomberg Industry Classification Standard Level 1.

To construct the capitalization-weighted index, this research sets 1 November 2019 as the base date of the index and aggregates the total market capitalization (i.e., stock price multiplied by the number of shares outstanding for all stocks excluding new initial public offerings and delistings) in each of the sector groups from each region. The total value is then converted to 1,000 (i.e., the starting level of the index) using a divisor. For each trading day after 1 November 2019, the market capitalization of the same groups of stocks is aggregated and divided by the same divisor to obtain the index level for that day. Since each stock's impact on the index value depends on its market capitalization, the daily price change in the index is therefore a capitalization-weighted return of all the stocks in the index. The data are collected from *Wind Information* for the PRC, and from Bloomberg LP for Hong Kong, China; ASEAN+2; and the rest of the world.

Figures B2.1, **B2.2**, and **B2.3** show how the stocks of different sectors in different regions performed from 1 November 2019 to 28 February 2020. Figure B2.1, which includes the sector indexes of the PRC and

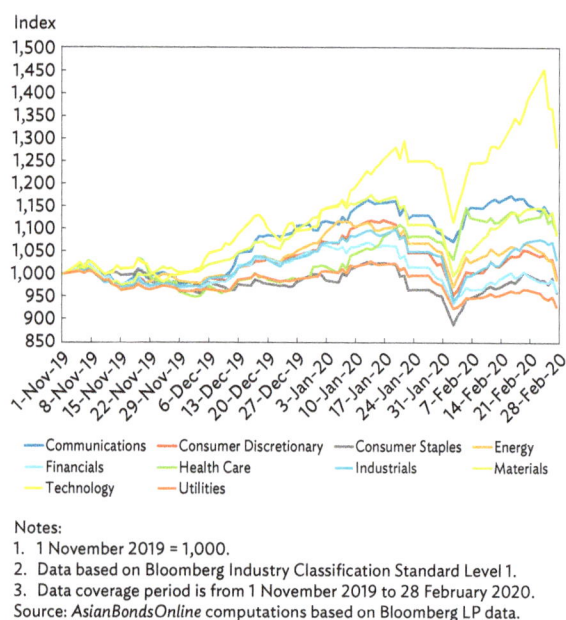

Figure B2.1: Sector-Level Stock Index Performances in the People's Republic of China and Hong Kong, China

Notes:
1. 1 November 2019 = 1,000.
2. Data based on Bloomberg Industry Classification Standard Level 1.
3. Data coverage period is from 1 November 2019 to 28 February 2020.
Source: *AsianBondsOnline* computations based on Bloomberg LP data.

Hong Kong, China, show sector-specific movements from 1 November 2019 until 20 January 2020. By late January, the indexes demonstrate strong comovement as the outbreak of COVID-19 further evolved, the government took nationwide measures to fight the outbreak, and the related negative impacts on economic activities became clearer. Such comovement was observed around each key COVID-19-related development through the first half of February. With gradual signs of the outbreak stabilizing within the PRC starting to appear in the middle of February, the sector indexes once again demonstrated more sector-specific movements until the last week of February when global stock markets dropped on negative sentiment driven by the rapid spread of COVID-19 outside of the PRC.

Figure B2.2 shows sector index performances in ASEAN+2 stock markets, which were broadly similar to those observed in the PRC and Hong Kong, China. Each sector largely tracked its sector-specific fundamentals from 1 November 2019 until the middle of January 2020. From late January until 19 February, the sector indexes reacted to COVID-19-related events, albeit with weaker reactions compared to those in the PRC and Hong Kong, China. However, as more COVID-19

---

[a] World Health Organization. COVID-19 Situation Report—40. 2020. https://www.who.int/docs/default-source/coronaviruse/situation-reports/20200229-sitrep-40-covid-19.pdf?sfvrsn=849d0665_2.

[b] This section presents general trends in the performances of different sector indexes in different regions. The designed index can also be affected by differences in trading rules such as different price limits and trading restrictions in different markets.

continued on next page

Box 2: How Are Financial Markets Reacting to the COVID-19 Outbreak? *continued*

Figure B2.2: Sector-Level Stock Index Performances in ASEAN, Japan, and the Republic of Korea

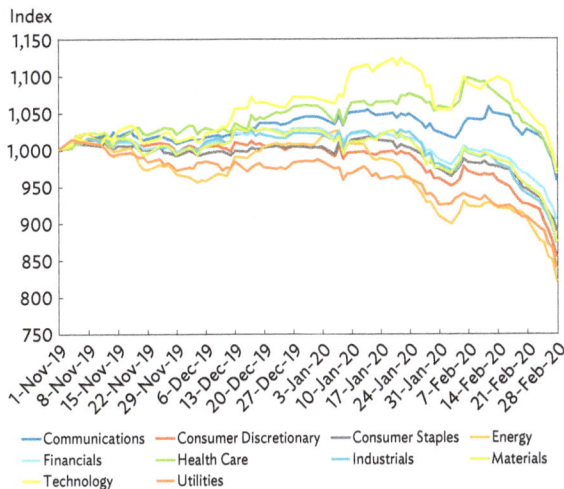

ASEAN = Association of Southeast Asian Nations.
Notes:
1. In this figure, ASEAN comprises Cambodia, Indonesia, the Lao People's Democratic Republic, Malaysia, the Philippines, Singapore, Thailand, and Viet Nam.
2. 1 November 2019 = 1,000.
3. Data based on Bloomberg Industry Classification Standard Level 1.
4. Data coverage period is from 1 November 2019 to 28 February 2020.
Source: *AsianBondsOnline* computations based on Bloomberg LP data.

Figure B2.3: Sector-Level Stock Index Performances in the Rest of the World

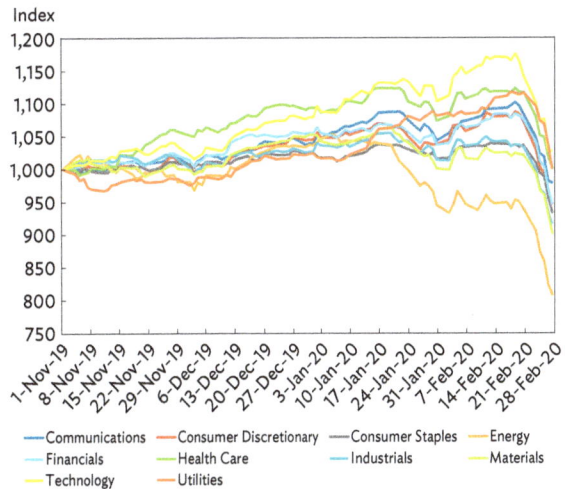

Notes:
1. In this figure, the rest of the world comprises Australia; Canada; Finland; France; Germany; India; Italy; the Russian Federation; Spain; Sri Lanka; Sweden; Taipei,China; and the United States.
2. 1 November 2019 = 1,000.
3. Data based on Bloomberg Industry Classification Standard Level 1.
4. Data coverage period is from 1 November 2019 to 28 February 2020.
Source: *AsianBondsOnline* computations based on Bloomberg LP data.

cases were confirmed in Japan and the Republic of Korea, sector stock indexes in ASEAN+2 experienced rapid declines from 20 February to 28 February.

Figure B2.3 shows the performance of stocks in the rest of the world during the same period. For the majority of the review period, these markets witnessed largely sector-specific movements with milder reactions to COVID-19-related news than occurred in the PRC and Hong Kong, China. However, stock markets in the rest of the world reacted strongly in late February amid a rapid rise in confirmed COVID-19 cases in some European and Middle East countries. The last week of February witnessed a major slump in global stock markets on the back of heightened risk aversion.

A detailed examination of sector returns is listed in **Table B2.1**, which reports the cumulative daily returns on the sector indexes of all three regions for 2-week periods from 1 January to 28 February. During the second half of January, stocks in the PRC and Hong Kong, China experienced market-wide declines in most sectors. Consumer discretionary and consumer staples posted the largest dips

at 8.5% and 7.0%, respectively. Stocks in ASEAN+2 and rest of the world were also negatively affected but to a milder extent. During the first 2 weeks of February, equity markets in the PRC and Hong Kong, China showed signs of stabilizing. During the last 2 weeks of February, with the number of confirmed cases outside the PRC and Hong Kong, China climbing fast, equity markets in ASEAN+2 and the rest of world experienced sharp declines. Markets in the PRC and Hong Kong, China were also affected by market contagion.

Table B2.2 compares the 2-month cumulative performance of sector indexes in all three regions. The results confirm that global equity markets reacted negatively to the outbreak of COVID-19 largely at the market level.

Overall, the trends suggest that (i) COVID-19 shocks to financial markets are largely occurring at the aggregate market-wide level; (ii) the reactions are related to investor sentiment, with more pronounced reactions to the COVID-19 outbreak in affected regions; and (iii) there were clear signs of equity market contagion during the last week of February when markets that had been stabilizing were weighed down by the global market slump.

continued on next page

Box 2: How Are Financial Markets Reacting to the COVID-19 Outbreak?   *continued*

Table B2.1: Sector Performance by Region

Period	1 Jan–15 Jan 2020			16 Jan–31 Jan 2020			1 Feb–15 Feb 2020			16 Feb–29 Feb 2020		
Sector	PRC + HKG	ASEAN+2	Rest of World	PRC + HKG	ASEAN+2	Rest of World	PRC + HKG	ASEAN+2	Rest of World	PRC + HKG	ASEAN+2	Rest of World
Communications	5.24	0.51	3.32	(5.75)	(2.50)	(2.88)	6.25	2.42	4.58	(6.01)	(8.84)	(10.77)
Consumer Discretionary	5.83	(0.97)	1.48	(8.46)	(3.33)	(2.16)	(0.33)	(0.28)	4.01	(2.00)	(11.29)	(12.88)
Consumer Staples	2.40	1.15	0.70	(7.00)	(3.98)	(1.57)	2.19	0.26	2.20	(1.11)	(9.29)	(10.49)
Energy	2.73	(1.79)	0.10	(4.32)	(8.17)	(9.26)	(0.26)	1.19	0.33	(5.13)	(11.22)	(15.60)
Financials	1.05	(1.05)	0.19	(6.80)	(3.07)	(1.88)	0.07	0.57	4.46	(2.75)	(9.43)	(13.43)
Health Care	4.04	0.06	2.16	1.33	(0.07)	(3.97)	4.27	1.48	4.14	(1.98)	(9.90)	(10.81)
Industrials	3.69	(0.23)	1.80	(4.46)	(3.77)	(2.95)	(1.47)	0.06	2.76	1.30	(11.63)	(12.72)
Materials	3.40	(1.15)	(0.10)	(5.62)	(3.81)	(4.86)	1.20	1.08	2.44	(1.48)	(11.87)	(12.66)
Technology	11.09	3.16	3.30	0.24	(4.65)	(1.02)	4.17	4.16	6.06	0.74	(12.65)	(12.87)
Utilities	2.83	(2.03)	2.09	(4.62)	(4.14)	3.44	(2.26)	(0.29)	2.48	(2.57)	(9.32)	(10.13)

( ) = negative; ASEAN = Association of Southeast Asian Nations; HKG = Hong Kong, China; PRC = People's Republic of China.
Notes:
1. In this table, ASEAN+2 comprises Cambodia, Indonesia, the Lao People's Democratic Republic, Malaysia, the Philippines, Singapore, Thailand, and Viet Nam plus Japan and the Republic of Korea.
2. The rest of the world comprises Australia; Canada; Finland; France; Germany; India; Italy; the Russian Federation; Spain; Sri Lanka; Sweden; Taipei,China; and the United States.
3. Data based on Bloomberg Industry Classification Standard Level 1.
Sources: *AsianBondsOnline* computations based on data from Bloomberg LP and *Wind Information*.

Table B2.2: Sector Performance by Region before and after the COVID-19 Outbreak

Period	1 Nov 2019–31 Dec 2019			1 Jan 2020–29 Feb 2020		
Sector	PRC + HKG	ASEAN+2	Rest of World	PRC + HKG	ASEAN+2	Rest of World
Communications	9.46	4.28	3.87	(0.26)	(8.41)	(5.75)
Consumer Discretionary	5.27	0.30	4.43	(4.97)	(15.86)	(9.55)
Consumer Staples	0.21	0.19	2.49	(3.51)	(11.85)	(9.17)
Energy	6.69	0.58	3.71	(6.97)	(19.99)	(24.44)
Financials	5.10	2.75	5.38	(8.42)	(12.97)	(10.65)
Health Care	1.93	5.74	8.98	7.66	(8.43)	(8.48)
Industrials	4.99	2.12	2.63	(0.95)	(15.57)	(11.12)
Materials	11.90	2.59	5.12	(2.50)	(15.75)	(15.18)
Technology	10.30	6.81	7.66	16.24	(9.97)	(4.54)
Utilities	(0.40)	(1.67)	2.33	(6.62)	(15.77)	(2.13)

( ) = negative; ASEAN = Association of Southeast Asian Nations; HKG = Hong Kong, China; PRC = People's Republic of China.
Notes:
1. In this table, ASEAN+2 comprises Cambodia, Indonesia, the Lao People's Democratic Republic, Malaysia, the Philippines, Singapore, Thailand, and Viet Nam plus Japan and the Republic of Korea.
2. The rest of the world comprises Australia; Canada; Finland; France; Germany; India; Italy; the Russian Federation; Spain; Sir Lanka; Sweden; Taipei,China; and the United States.
3. Data based on Bloomberg Industry Classification Standard Level 1.
Sources: *AsianBondsOnline* computations based on data from Bloomberg LP and *Wind Information*.

To reconfirm that equity markets are responding to COVID-19-related news at the market level, we conduct a focus group comparison based on relevant geographical factors. For the PRC market, we construct two similar capitalization-weighted indexes using the stocks of firms located in Hubei Province (Hubei Index) and Wuhan City (Wuhan Index). The performances of these two indexes are compared with the Shanghai–Shenzhen 300 (CSI 300)

Index over the same period. In the United States (US) market, we formed a similar capitalization-weighted index of US-listed Chinese companies and compared it with the Standard and Poor's 500 (S&P 500) Index. **Figure B2.4** shows the movements of all five of these indexes. While the Hubei Index and the Wuhan Index largely tracked the CSI 300 Index, albeit with some idiosyncratic movements prior to 20 January, the Hubei Index and the Wuhan Index

continued on next page

Box 2: How Are Financial Markets Reacting to the COVID-19 Outbreak?   *continued*

Figure B2.4: Stock Index Performances for Select Locations and Major Indexes

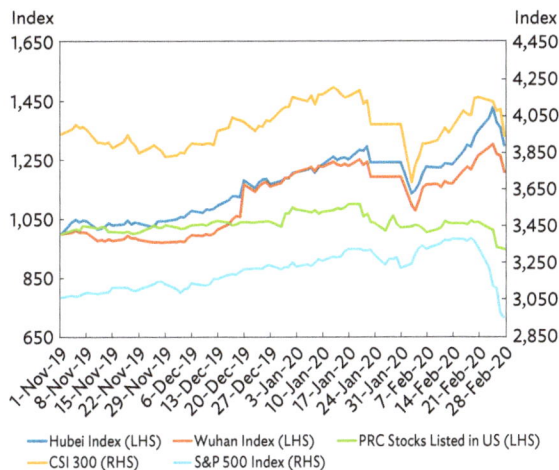

CSI 300 = Shanghai–Shenzhen China Securities Index, LHS = left-hand side, PRC = People's Republic of China, RHS = right-hand side, S&P 500 = Standard & Poor's Index, US = United States.
Notes:
1. 1 November 2019 = 1,000.
2. Data coverage period is from 1 November 2019 to 28 February 2020.
Source: *Wind Information* and Bloomberg LP.

Figure B2.5: Stock Index Performances for Selected Sectors across Regions

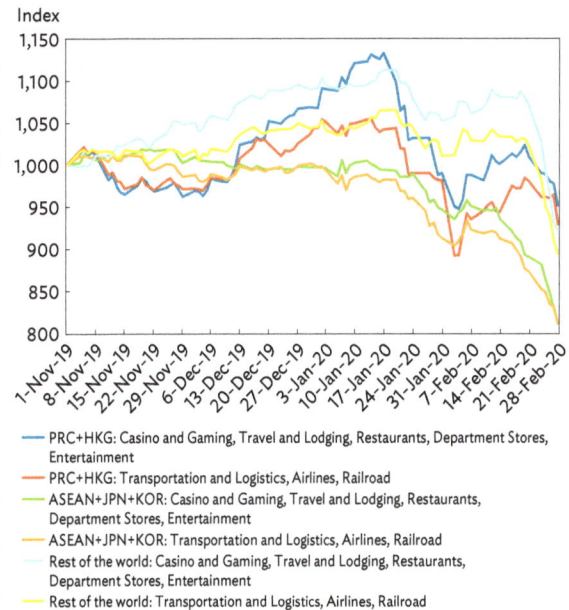

ASEAN = Association of Southeast Asian Nations; HKG = Hong Kong, China; JPN = Japan; KOR = Republic of Korea; PRC = People's Republic of China.
Notes:
1. In this figure, ASEAN comprises Cambodia, Malaysia, the Philippines, Singapore, Thailand, and Viet Nam.
2. In this figure, the rest of the world comprises Australia; Canada; Finland; France; Germany; India; Italy; the Russian Federation; Spain; Sri Lanka; Sweden; Taipei,China; and the United States.
3. 1 November 2019 = 1,000.
4. Data based on Bloomberg Industry Classification Standard Level 2 breakdown.
5. Data coverage period is from 1 November 2019 to 28 February 2020.
Source: *AsianBondsOnline* computations based on Bloomberg LP data.

started to comove more closely with the CSI 300 Index after 20 January in response to COVID-19-related news. In the US market, the stocks of Chinese companies closely tracked the movement of the S&P 500 Index and showed limited reaction to COVID-19-related news until 20 February. However, amid the market slump during the last 10 days of February, the stocks of US-listed Chinese companies were, to a lesser extent, negatively affected by the plunging S&P 500 Index. Notably, these stocks did not follow the market trend in the PRC, where stock prices were picking up as the global slump started. These two comparisons further demonstrate that equity market reactions to the outbreak have tended to occur at the market level.

To reconfirm that COVID-19 shocks affect markets where concerns over an outbreak are more pronounced, we focused on stocks from two Bloomberg Industry Classification Systems Level 2 sectors that are most likely to be affected by COVID-19-related developments. These are (i) casino and gaming, travel and lodging, restaurants, department stores, and entertainment (Leisure Index); and (ii) transportation and logistics, airlines, and railroads (Logistics Index). As **Figure B2.5** shows, from 20 January to 5 February, when the PRC was the most affected market, both the Leisure Index and the Logistics Index suffered larger declines in the PRC

and Hong Kong, China than in the other two regions included in the study. From 14 February to 21 February, the Leisure and Logistics Indexes suffered the largest declines in ASEAN+2 markets, as Japan and the Republic of Korea experienced an increase in confirmed cases. However, from 21 February—when Europe, the Middle East, and the US began reporting an increase in COVID-19 cases—equity markets in the rest of world reacted sharply as global markets experienced a contagion of fear during the last week of February.

In sum, equity markets' reactions to COVID-19-related news have been quite intuitive. First, equity markets reacted to such information largely at the market level. Second, the reaction was most pronounced in markets where the number of COVID-19 cases rose quickly. Third, when COVID-19 spread to the global economy, global equity markets experienced contagion during the ensuing market slump.

Figure F: Foreign Holdings of Local Currency Government Bonds in Select Asian Markets (% of total)

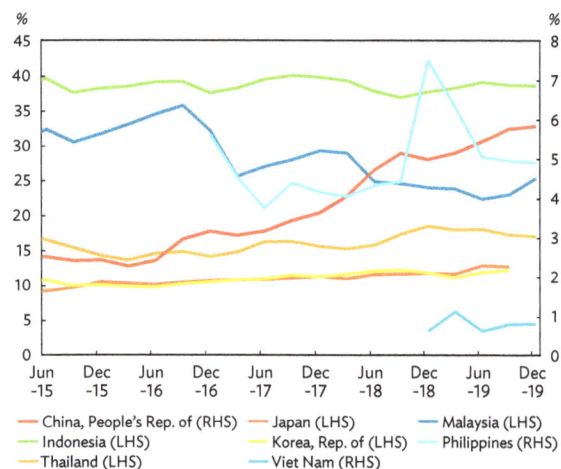

LHS = left-hand side, RHS = right-hand side.
Note: Data as of 31 December 2019 except for Japan and the Republic of Korea (30 September 2019).
Source: *AsianBondsOnline*.

countries that have suffered a major outbreak of the disease. The behavioral changes induced by the disease—such as not going to restaurants, shopping centers, or cinemas—will dampen domestic demand. Leisure and hospitality industries, including domestic demand, will also suffer. Second, international travel and tourism is bound to suffer as a result of travel restrictions imposed on flights originating in or transiting through COVID-19 hotspots. Even in the absence of restrictions, tourists and business travelers alike will postpone or cancel plans as a precautionary measure against becoming infected. Given the PRC's large and growing importance as a source of international tourists, countries where tourism is an important part of the economy will be hit especially hard. Finally, trade and production linkages are another source of spillovers. The slowdown of the PRC's economic growth will reduce the exports of other countries to the PRC. Given the PRC's central role in regional production networks, production disruptions in the PRC will reverberate across East and Southeast Asian economies with which the PRC has close trade and other economic linkages.

There are other channels through which COVID-19 can adversely affect economic performance. For example, weak business confidence can harm investment. This is especially true if the disease persists for an extended period of time, thereby harming long-term economic prospects. Most estimates of the negative economic impact of COVID-19 on the PRC's GDP range from 0.3 to 1.7 percentage points in 2020. That is, if the PRC would have grown by 5.9% in 2020 in the absence of the disease, growth of between 4.2% and 5.6% is now expected. Such an impact is substantial by any measure. Furthermore, the spillover effects from the PRC's slowdown will slow growth in the rest of the region and the world.

The negative impact of the disease will not only be limited to the real economy but also be felt in financial markets. For example, as a result of the rapid increase in the number of infections in the Republic of Korea since the middle of February, the won–dollar rate briefly fell below the psychologically significant 1,200-to-1 mark. In addition, equity markets in the region and the rest of the world are reacting to news about the disease. The effect of the disease on the real economy and financial markets are not independent of each other. In particular, the weakening of the real economy will harm the performance of firms and jeopardize their ability

and beyond to reach 85,403 and 2,924, respectively, as of 29 February.[3] While the overwhelming majority of cases have been in the PRC, especially Hubei province, a number of other countries, most notably the Republic of Korea, Iran, and Italy have also suffered major outbreaks. By the end of February, the number of cases seemed to be stabilizing in the PRC while growing rapidly in the rest of the world. Much remains unknown about the disease, including the maximum incubation period, which is adding to the general public's fear and panic. It is too early to tell when COVID-19 will be contained and brought under control. The highly infectious nature of the disease has led to a contagion of fear affecting many individuals across the PRC, Asia, and other regions. This contagion of fear has been amplified by social media, which barely existed during the SARS outbreak, a broadly similar outbreak that originated in the PRC in 2003. Although highly infectious, the fatality rate of COVID-19 appears to be relatively low at 1.0%–2.0%.

Given the contagious nature of COVID-19 and the contagion of fear it has spawned, the disease is likely to have sizable economic effects. There are at least three major channels through which the disease will adversely affect economies. First, consumption and retail sales are likely to take a major hit as consumers refrain from going out. This will be especially true in the PRC and other

[3] World Health Organization. COVID-19 Situation Report—40. 2020. https://www.who.int/docs/default-source/coronaviruse/situation-reports/20200229-sitrep-40-covid-19.pdf?sfvrsn=849d0665_2.

to repay debts. This, in turn, will saddle banks with bad loans, damaging their balance sheets and thus threatening the soundness and stability of the banking system. The negative effect of COVID-19 on the real economy and financial markets became more pronounced during the first 2 weeks of March. Global oil prices and global stock markets fell sharply, reflecting growing concerns about a global pandemic.

Although COVID-19 is by far the biggest downside risk to global growth and financial stability, it is by no means the only one. In particular, PRC–US trade tensions continue to pose a major threat. The Phase 1 deal agreed upon by the two economic giants is clearly a welcome development. It binds them to fulfill specific commitments through the end of 2020 and thus makes it unlikely that new disputes will arise this year. Yet, the trade conflict awaits a comprehensive, systematic resolution. In the absence of a long-term fundamental agreement, the conflict will remain a significant source of uncertainty for the world economy and global financial markets. Other risks include geopolitical risks associated with tensions in the Middle East. If those tensions are not defused and instead escalate into direct conflict, the outcome may be a serious disruption in the flow of oil from the region to the rest of the world.

Despite the short-term challenge posted by COVID-19, emerging East Asia continues to pursue an agenda of sustainable development, which can help mitigate the negative effects of climate change and global warming. Green bonds serve as an effective instrument to finance environment-friendly investments such as cleaner power plants. At the same time, green bonds can contribute to bond market development in the region as policy makers and regulators level the playing field for the issuance of such bonds. Specifically, a bond market regulatory framework, including issuance and trading mechanisms, would benefit from green bond market development (**Box 3**). On the demand side, environmental, social, and governance investing has become increasingly popular among the global asset management community. Existing evidence shows that such investments can deliver good returns (**Box 4**).

Box 3: Green Bond Quantitative Performance during Periods of Market Stress— 2020 Update

Introduction

Green bonds can be an effective market-based approach to financing climate solutions for investors with sustainable investment mandates. But the potential existence of a "greenium" is a significant hindrance to conventional investors buying these bonds as a mainstream investment, as they have to justify any reduction in spread compensation from a risk-and-return perspective, consistent with their own fiduciary duty. If, however, a "green factor" exists for green bonds that sustainably delivers superior risk-adjusted returns and/or exhibit downside risk protection—qualities that investors can assign a value to—then a greenium may be explainable from a fundamental market-pricing perspective. To test this hypothesis, we analyzed the secondary market performance of green bonds versus conventional equivalents to isolate the green factor and test for a relationship with secondary market performance.

This update extends our prior research to include analysis of green bonds' relative performance in both the United States (US) dollar and euro markets, with new findings and an expanded data set to make comparisons between regions.

Performance of Green vs. Conventional Bond Equivalents: Total Returns of EUR-Denominated Bond Baskets Matched for Sector, Currency, Liquidity, Issuance Vintage, Size, and Country Risk

First, we compared the total return performance of matched baskets of green and conventional bonds in the same sector to isolate the green factor as a driver of returns by controlling for idiosyncratic factors. We created baskets of all EUR-denominated, green-labeled and conventional, non-hybrid, fixed-rate, benchmark-sized bonds issued between April 2016 and September 2017 by European-domiciled, investment-grade-rated, power utility companies. The average duration, credit rating, and spread level of the baskets at the start of the review period were similar. Liquidity was considered equivalent because all bonds in the sample were issued in the same period, and the average notional value of the green bond basket at EUR675 million was larger than the EUR560 million average notional value of the conventional equivalent basket. Because the underlying country composition of issuers in the baskets differed, we made two versions of the conventional bond basket to account for country risk: (i) one with as-issued country weights and (ii) another with country

continued on next page

Box 3: Green Bond Quantitative Performance during Periods of Market Stress— 2020 Update   *continued*

weights equalized to that of the green bond basket to account for intra-euro area country risk.

The total returns of the green bond basket outperformed the conventional bond baskets, both the as-issued and equalized country-weight versions, by 90 basis points (bps) and 48 bps, respectively, between 1 October 2017 and 11 July 2018. The green bond basket's outperformance became most pronounced in May 2018, coinciding with a period of general market volatility following elections in Italy (**Figure B3.1**).

Figure B3.1: Performance of Green vs. Conventional Bonds—Total Returns of EUR-Denominated Bond Baskets Matched for Sector, Currency, and Liquidity

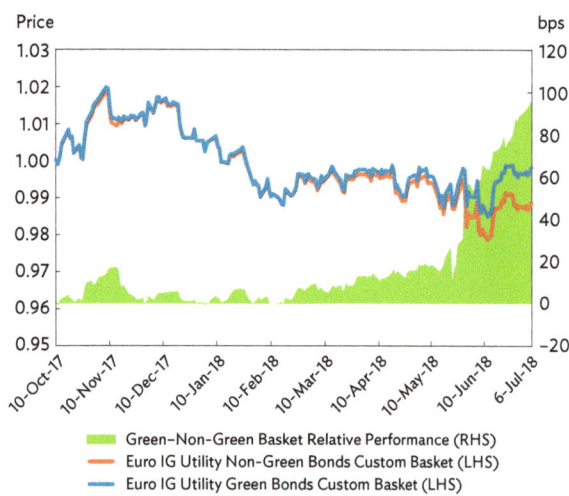

bps = basis points, LHS = left-hand side, RHS = right-hand side.
Source: Nomura Asset Management calculations.

Additionally, we tested if the green factor's performance effect extended beyond individually labeled green bonds to all of the issuer's new bonds, regardless of label. We classified all corporate issuers as either a green bond issuer if they had at least one green bond outstanding between April 2016 and September 2017, or as a non-green bond issuers if they did not. We then constructed matched baskets of all newly issued bonds as before. The green bond issuer basket outperformed the non-green bond issuer basket by 42 bps when using as-issued country weights and by 49 bps with equalized country weights, again mainly during the period of market volatility in and around May 2018. This indicates that the green factor may enhance the issuer's overall credit profile. This seems reasonable, as the act of issuing even a single green bond

requires top-level management buy-in and a commitment to sustainability, data collection, transparency, and reporting in a way that extends through the entire organization.

Performance Analysis of Green vs. Non-Green: Relative Performance of EUR-Denominated and USD-Denominated Corporate Bonds of the Same Issuer Curve in Periods of Credit Market Stress

We then analyzed the relative spread performance of green versus conventional bonds at the issuer level to control for non-green idiosyncratic factors in both the euro and dollar markets. We calculated the individual performance of each green and conventional bond relative to fair value for that issuer's liquid curve, using discrete periods of generalized credit market volatility as natural experiments to shock the EUR- and USD-denominated corporate credit curves across issuers. For pricing data, we used periods of credit market volatility and spread widening in May–June 2018 following the Italian elections for the EUR-denominated bond analysis and October–December 2018 during a 20% sell-off in S&P 500 stocks for the USD-denominated bond analysis.

Method of Analysis

For the EUR-denominated green bond analysis, we selected 14 European investment-grade banks and utility companies with liquid, fixed-rate, non-hybrid credit curves and at least one liquid green bond (minimum size EUR500 million, average size EUR750 million). We calculated fair value yield curves for each issuer using regression analysis. We calculated each bond's difference (in bps) from the fair value curve on 16 May 2018, which was 2 weeks before the peak in spread widening, or "T-2w," and again on the new equilibrium shocked curve as of 20 June 2018, which was 3 weeks after the peak in spread widening, or "T+3w." We defined performance as the net change in a bond's spread to fair value (in bps residual) from T-2w to T+3w (**Figure B3.2**). For example, the Intesa Sanpaolo 2022 (ISPIM 0.875% 6/2022) green bond was 0.4 bps wide (cheap) to the fair value curve at T-2w and 4.8 bps tight (rich) to the curve on T+3w, implying 5.2 bps of net tightening (richening) (**Figure B3.3**). As the sum of all bond fair-value residuals sums to zero, this method ensured internal consistency and comparability across issuers.

For the USD-denominated green bond analysis, we identified nine US investment-grade financial corporations and energy utilities with liquid, fixed-rate, non-hybrid credit curves and at

continued on next page

Box 3: Green Bond Quantitative Performance during Periods of Market Stress— 2020 Update *continued*

Figure B3.2: EUR-Denominated Aggregate Corporate OAS and Italy 5-Year CDS

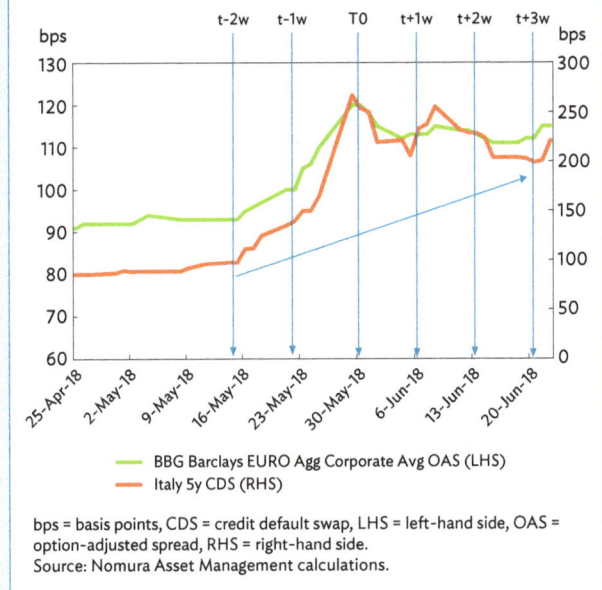

BBG Barclays EURO Agg Corporate Avg OAS (LHS)
Italy 5y CDS (RHS)

bps = basis points, CDS = credit default swap, LHS = left-hand side, OAS = option-adjusted spread, RHS = right-hand side.
Source: Nomura Asset Management calculations.

Figure B3.3: ISPIM—Intesa Sanpaolo SpA Bank (Italy)

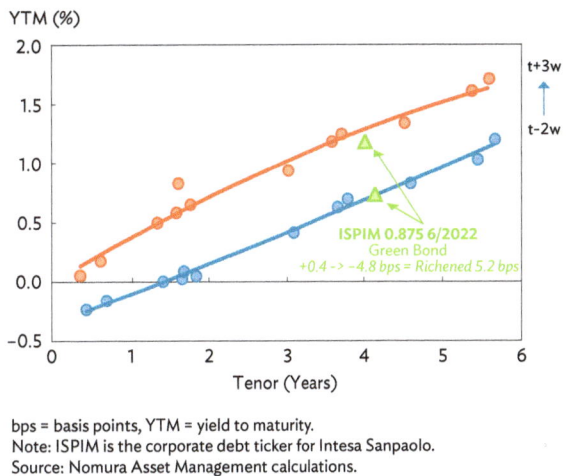

ISPIM 0.875 6/2022
Green Bond
+0.4 -> -4.8 bps = Richened 5.2 bps

bps = basis points, YTM = yield to maturity.
Note: ISPIM is the corporate debt ticker for Intesa Sanpaolo.
Source: Nomura Asset Management calculations.

least one liquid green bond (minimum size USD300 million, average size USD605 million). We calculated fair value curves and the degree of divergence for each issuer and bond in the same manner as the EUR-denominated sample. We used start and end dates based on the trough and peak of US dollar market credit spreads from 3 October 2018 to 2 January 2019, because in this case the market immediately recovered after the sell-off without any well-defined new equilibrium level ever being established. As in the EUR-denominated bond analysis, performance was calculated as the net change in the fair value residual at the start and end points of the observation period.

Analysis Results and Discussion

During the respective sample periods, EUR-denominated green bonds on average outperformed conventional bonds on the same issuer curve (i.e., spreads tightened) by an average of 1.5 bps, while USD-denominated green bonds outperformed conventional bonds by an average of 2.8 bps. The average green bond outperformance for the combined EUR-denominated and USD-denominated bond market sample was 2.0 bps. The pattern of outperformance of green bond relative returns at the issuer level was asymmetrically distributed, with a skew of 1.0 bp of outperformance across the EUR-denominated and USD-denominated samples. In

other words, green bonds tended to either perform the same or outperform conventional bonds during periods of market stress (**Table B3.1**).

Green bonds, whether denominated in euros or US dollars, showed a consistent pattern of outperformance during the review period against conventional bonds with respect to industry sector and credit rating (**Table B3.2**). The average outperformance of green bonds in the utilities sector (euros 2.7 bps, US dollars 3.6 bps) was greater than in the financial sector (euros 0.8 bps, US dollars 1.3 bps). Furthermore, the degree of both EUR- and USD-denominated green bond outperformance showed a strong correlation with decreasing credit ratings (i.e., the riskier the credit, the more green bonds outperformed on the same issuer's curve.) This may reflect market-implied relative materiality across segments; that is, "greenness" is more highly valued among utility credits than financial credits, and among lower-rated credits than higher-rated credits.

Specific to the EUR-denominated bond sample where intra-euro area country risk is present, a significant factor explaining the degree of green bond outperformance for any particular issuer in the sample regardless of sector is whether the issuer was an Italian company (**Table B3.3**). Enel SpA (integrated energy utility) and Intesa Sanpaolo SpA (bank) on average experienced the largest green vs. conventional bond relative performance gaps in the EUR-denominated sample at 8.3 bps and 5.2 bps, respectively. In this case, the green bond outperformance effect—or downside risk resiliency—was

continued on next page

Box 3: Green Bond Quantitative Performance during Periods of Market Stress— 2020 Update *continued*

Table B3.1: Issuer Average Green Bond Performance Relative to Non-Green Bonds

A. EUR-Denominated Green Bonds

Issuer Name	Debt Ticker	Credit Rating Band	Sector	Average Green Bond Relative Performance, T–2w to T+3w (bps)	Country
Enel	ENELIM	BBB	Utilities	(8.3)	Italy
Intesa Sanpaolo	ISPIM	BBB	Financial	(5.2)	Italy
EDF	EDF	A	Utilities	(4.0)	France
Tennet	TENN	A	Utilities	(1.3)	Netherlands
SocGen	SOCGEN	A	Financial	(1.3)	France
BBVA	BBVASM	A	Financial	(0.9)	Spain
Engie	ENGIFP	A	Utilities	(0.5)	France
Berlin Hypo	BHH	A	Financial	(0.4)	Germany
ABN Amro	ABNANV	A	Financial	(0.3)	Netherlands
NRW Bank	NRWBK	AA	Financial	(0.2)	Germany
ING	INTNED	A	Financial	0.3	Netherlands
KfW	KFW	AAA	Financial	0.5	Germany
Iberdrola	IBESM	BBB	Utilities	0.5	Spain
BNP	BNP	A	Financial	0.6	France

B. USD-Denominated Green Bonds

Issuer Name	Debt Ticker	Credit Rating Band	Sector	Average Green Bond Relative Performance from Trough to Peak (bps)
Southern Power Co	SO	BBB	Utilities	(7.0)
Public Service Co of Colorado	XEL	A	Utilities	(5.2)
Interstate Power and Light	LNT	BBB	Utilities	(5.1)
Alexandria Real Estate Properties	ARE	BBB	Financial	(4.1)
DTE Electric Co	DTE	A	Utilities	(3.7)
MidAmerican Energy	BRKHEC	AA	Utilities	(0.3)
Bank of America Corp	BAC	A	Financial	(0.3)
Westar Energy	EVRG	A	Utilities	(0.3)
Digital Realty Trust	DLR	BBB	Financial	0.3

( ) = negative.
Note: A negative figure indicates net spread tightening (i.e., outperformance by the issuer's green bonds).
Source: Nomura Asset Management calculations.

largest for the issuers most exposed to the underlying driver of the sell-off (i.e., Italian sovereign risk).

Is a Greenium Justifiable as an "Insurance Premium"?

These results support the view that green bonds can deliver superior risk-adjusted performance with downside risk protection and that this may be attributable to a green factor after controlling for idiosyncratic variables. The expanded performance data show evidence of a market-implied green factor materiality that differs with respect to sector and credit rating, but not currency. Furthermore, this green factor extends to all of an issuer's newly issued bonds, possibly implying that a commitment to green bond issuance can itself be an indicator of superior sustainability and/or governance, which are important factors for investors pursuing environmental-, social-, and governance-integrated strategies. If true, we postulate that the market may eventually come to justify some degree of a greenium as a fundamental quality factor, like an "insurance premium" with intrinsic value, thereby supporting sustainable growth in the green bond market.

continued on next page

Box 3: Green Bond Quantitative Performance during Periods of Market Stress—2020 Update   *continued*

Table B3.2: Cross-Sector Analysis of Green Bond Relative Performance by Currency, Credit Rating Band, and Sector

	Utilities	Financial	All	AAA	AA	A	BBB
EUR	(2.7)	(0.8)	(1.5)	0.5	(0.2)	(0.9)	(4.3)
USD	(3.6)	(1.3)	(2.8)		(0.3)	(2.4)	(3.9)
All Currencies	(3.2)	(0.9)	(2.0)	0.5	(0.3)	(1.3)	(4.1)

	Utilities	Financial	All	EUR	USD
AAA		0.5	0.5	0.5	
AA	(0.3)	(0.2)	(0.3)	(0.2)	(0.3)
A	(2.5)	(0.3)	(1.3)	(0.9)	(2.4)
BBB	(4.9)	(3.0)	(4.1)	(4.3)	(3.9)
All Ratings	(3.2)	(0.9)	(2.0)	(1.5)	(2.8)

	EUR	USD	All	AAA	AA	A	BBB
Utilities	(2.7)	(3.6)	(3.2)		(0.3)	(2.5)	(4.9)
Financial	(0.8)	(1.3)	(0.9)	0.5	(0.2)	(0.3)	(3.0)
All Sectors	(1.5)	(2.8)	(2.0)	0.5	(0.3)	(1.3)	(4.1)

( ) = negative, EUR = euro, USD = United States dollar.
Note: A negative figure indicates net spread tightening (i.e., outperformance by green bonds).
Source: Nomura Asset Management calculations.

Table B3.3: EUR-Denominated Green Bond Relative Performance by Country of Risk

	Utilities	Financial	All	AAA	AA	A	BBB
Italy	(8.3)	(5.2)	(6.7)				(6.7)
France	(2.2)	(0.3)	(1.3)			(1.3)	
Netherlands	(1.3)	0.0	(0.4)			(0.4)	
Spain	0.5	(0.9)	(0.2)			(0.9)	0.5
Germany		(0.1)	(0.1)	0.5	(0.2)	(0.4)	
All Countries	(2.7)	(0.8)	(1.5)	0.5	(0.2)	(0.9)	(4.3)

( ) = negative.
Note: A negative figure indicates net spread tightening (i.e., outperformance by green bonds).
Source: Nomura Asset Management calculations.

Box 4: The Alpha and Beta of ESG Investing

With rising awareness of environmental, social, and governance (ESG) issues worldwide, responsible investing has gained considerable traction, particularly in Europe and North America during the past 5 years. In 2018, Amundi, Europe's largest asset manager and a pioneer in responsible investment, researched the impact of ESG investment criteria on portfolio performance.[a] Amundi's research on the impact of ESG investing on equity asset pricing found that when an alpha strategy is massively implemented, it becomes a beta strategy. In Europe, the massive mobilization of institutional investors pursuing ESG investing has impacted demand mechanisms, with a subsequent effect on prices, thereby also triggering a performance premium.

According to Amundi's findings, 2014 marked a turning point as ESG screening drove an outperformance in developed market equities, with a strong impact on environmental investment in North America and governance investment in the euro area. While ESG investing generally tended to penalize both passive and active investors between 2010 and 2013, ESG investing was a source of outperformance from 2014 to 2017 in both Europe and North America. For example, buying the best-in-class (20% best-ranked) stocks and selling the worst-in-class (20% worst-ranked) stocks would have generated an annualized return of 3.3% in North America and 6.6% in the euro area during the period 2014–2017, while these figures were, respectively, –2.70% and –1.20% during the period 2010–2013.

Among the three ESG pillars, the environmental pillar in North America and the governance pillar in the euro area performed the strongest. From 2016, the social component improved significantly and is now being positively priced by the stock market. Overall, the study revealed that ESG investing does not impact all stocks, but rather it tends to impact best-in-class and worst-in-class assets.

In a 2019 update, Amundi confirmed its earlier findings and identified the following additional trends:

- **Transatlantic divide.** After 8 years of consistency, we observed a divergence between North America and the euro area in ESG equity trends. In North America, there was a decrease in alpha generation in all

three dimensions in 2019, and even a loss in the environmental pillar. In the euro area, the same positive dynamic still operated with the environmental and social pillars outperforming. For example, buying the best-in-class ESG stocks and selling the worst-in-class ESG stocks would have generated an annualized return of 5.8% in the euro area but only 0.6% in North America (versus 6.6.% and 3.3% for the period 2014–2017).

- **Social: From laggard to leader.** From 2010 to 2017, the social pillar's integration lagged when compared with the environmental and governance pillars. However, since 2018, social has been the best-performing pillar. When a portfolio took a long position in the 20% of best-ranked stocks and a short position in the 20% of worst-ranked stocks, this led to an annualized return of 2.9% in the euro area and 1.6% in North America. Similarly, optimized index management, in which the weighting of companies in the index is optimized to obtain the lowest possible tracking error, would have created an excess return of about 60 basis points (bps) and 40 bps in the euro area and North America, respectively, for a tracking error of 50 bps. We believe this resulted from more sustainable investors exploring the latest trends in ESG investing amid rising interest in social themes.

- **ESG investing: Growing in complexity.** Our study shows that ESG investing goes beyond the exclusion of worst-in-class stocks or the selection of best-in-class stocks.[b] We found that the growing relationship between ESG ranking and performance is sometimes affected by the behavior of second-to-worst-in-class stocks. We hypothesize that the abnormal performance of these stocks is due to the development of forward-looking strategies, with some investors betting on improving companies instead of well-scored companies. We argue that the emergence of ESG momentum strategies and the shift toward a dynamic view of ESG ratings is a positive development, as it reinforces the complexity of ESG integration. This demonstrates that sustainable investors might better understand underlying issues and are moving beyond a binary view of corporations.

---

[a] The updated study, *ESG Investing in Recent Years: New Insights from Old Challenges*, and the original seminal paper, *The Alpha and Beta of ESG Investing*, can be found on the webpage of the Amundi Research Center at http://research-center.amundi.com.The latest research is based on quantitative data from January 2018 to June 2019 using ESG metrics provided by the Amundi ESG Research Department. For each company, the overall ESG score and the ratings for the separate environmental, social, and governance categories were assessed by Amundi ESG analysts, who rated each stock using a scoring system determined by four external providers. Amundi ESG analysts reviewed and finalized the score of each company.

[b] Second-to-worst in class stocks: This research divides the stocks into five quintiles according to their ESG score. Those in the worst-in-class category (fifth quintile) are the 20% of stocks with the lowest ESG score. The second-to-worst-in-class stocks are those in the fourth quintile.

continued on next page

Box 4: The Alpha and Beta of ESG Investing *continued*

In conclusion, ESG investing is rapidly evolving. In 2016, the size of the global responsible investment market was USD22.9 trillion. Two years later, it stood at USD30.7 trillion (**Table B4**). While the ESG investing space is becoming more complex—for example, environmental policy reversals in the United States, a shift from a static to dynamic view of ESG scores, lead and lag integration of the different dimensions—our results show that the ESG fundamentals are still present. Best-in-class and worst-in-class approaches still work overall, and this is good news on the investment side.

Table B4: Size and Growth of Global Responsible Investment Markets

Markets	Size (USD trillion)	Growth in 2 Years (%)	Market Share (%)
Australia and New Zealand	0.7	46	2
Canada	1.7	42	6
Europe	14.1	11	46
Japan	2.2	364	7
United States	12.0	38	39
Total	30.7	34	100

Source: Global Sustainable Investment Alliance (2019).

Bond Market Developments in the Fourth Quarter of 2019

Size and Composition

Emerging East Asia's local currency bonds outstanding reached USD16.0 trillion at the end of December despite a slowdown in growth in most markets in the region in Q4 2019.

The outstanding amount of local currency (LCY) bonds in emerging East Asia totaled USD16.0 trillion at the end of December.[4] While remaining positive, overall growth softened to 2.4% quarter-on-quarter (q-o-q) in the fourth quarter (Q4) of 2019 from 3.1% q-o-q in the third (Q3) quarter (**Figure 1a**). Growth was capped by a slowdown in the issuance of government bonds in Q4 2019 as a number of governments had already completed their borrowing plans for the year. The q-o-q growth rate of bonds outstanding moderated between

Q3 2019 and Q4 2019 in seven out of the region's nine bond markets. Only the bond markets of Thailand and Hong Kong, China saw faster q-o-q expansions in Q4 2019.

Emerging East Asia's bond market growth also moderated on a year-on-year (y-o-y) basis, easing to 12.5% in Q4 2019 from 13.0% in Q3 2019 (**Figure 1b**). Excluding the bond markets of the Republic of Korea, Singapore, and Viet Nam, all emerging East Asian bond markets posted a slowdown in y-o-y growth in Q4 2019 versus the preceding quarter.

The People's Republic of China (PRC) remained the region's leader in terms of size, with its outstanding bond stock expanding to USD12,090.0 billion at the end of December. The PRC's LCY bond market accounted

---

Figure 1a: Growth of Local Currency Bond Markets in the Third and Fourth Quarters of 2019 (q-o-q, %)

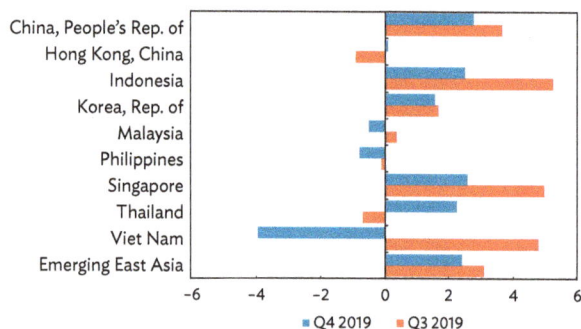

q-o-q = quarter-on-quarter, Q3 = third quarter, Q4 = fourth quarter.
Notes:
1. Calculated using data from national sources.
2. Growth rates are calculated from local currency base and do not include currency effects.
3. Emerging East Asia growth figures are based on 31 December 2019 currency exchange rates and do not include currency effects.
4. For Singapore, corporate bonds outstanding are based on *AsianBondsOnline* estimates.
5. For Hong Kong, China, the data series for corporate bonds outstanding was revised starting in 2018 to include more short-term debt securities.
Sources: People's Republic of China (CEIC); Hong Kong, China (Hong Kong Monetary Authority); Indonesia (Bank Indonesia; Directorate General of Budget Financing and Risk Management, Ministry of Finance; and Indonesia Stock Exchange); Republic of Korea (*EDAILY BondWeb* and The Bank of Korea); Malaysia (Bank Negara Malaysia); Philippines (Bureau of the Treasury and Bloomberg LP); Singapore (Monetary Authority of Singapore, Singapore Government Securities, and Bloomberg LP); Thailand (Bank of Thailand); and Viet Nam (Bloomberg LP and Vietnam Bond Market Association).

Figure 1b: Growth of Local Currency Bond Markets in the Third and Fourth Quarters of 2019 (y-o-y, %)

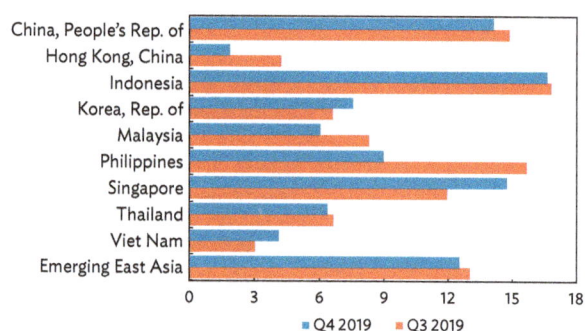

Q3 = third quarter, Q4 = fourth quarter, y-o-y = year-on-year.
Notes:
1. Calculated using data from national sources.
2. Growth rates are calculated from local currency base and do not include currency effects.
3. Emerging East Asia growth figures are based on 31 December 2019 currency exchange rates and do not include currency effects.
4. For Singapore, corporate bonds outstanding are based on *AsianBondsOnline* estimates.
5. For Hong Kong, China, the data series for corporate bonds outstanding was revised starting in 2018 to include more short-term debt securities.
Sources: People's Republic of China (CEIC); Hong Kong, China (Hong Kong Monetary Authority); Indonesia (Bank Indonesia; Directorate General of Budget Financing and Risk Management, Ministry of Finance; and Indonesia Stock Exchange); Republic of Korea (*EDAILY BondWeb* and The Bank of Korea); Malaysia (Bank Negara Malaysia); Philippines (Bureau of the Treasury and Bloomberg LP); Singapore (Monetary Authority of Singapore, Singapore Government Securities, and Bloomberg LP); Thailand (Bank of Thailand); and Viet Nam (Bloomberg LP and Vietnam Bond Market Association).

---

[4] Emerging East Asia comprises the People's Republic of China; Hong Kong, China; Indonesia; the Republic of Korea; Malaysia; the Philippines; Singapore; Thailand; and Viet Nam.

for a 75.4% share of emerging East Asian total bonds outstanding at the end of December, up from 75.2% at the end of September. Growth in the PRC's bond market eased to 2.8% q-o-q in Q4 2019 from 3.6% q-o-q in the preceding quarter.

Overall growth in the PRC's bond market was pulled down by government bonds, which grew 2.0% q-o-q in Q4 2019 versus 3.5% q-o-q in Q3 2019. In particular, growth in the stock of local government bonds plunged to 0.4% q-o-q in Q4 2019 from 5.1% q-o-q in Q3 2019. Quotas for issuing local government bonds had been mostly met by the end of September, resulting in a relatively small volume of issuance in Q4 2019. In the first 3 quarters of the year, local government bonds were the major growth driver in the PRC's government bond segment.

On the other hand, the corporate bond segment grew at a slightly faster pace of 4.1% q-o-q in Q4 2019, up from 3.9% q-o-q in the prior quarter. The growth in the corporate bond stock was fueled by increased bond issuance from private enterprises and offerings of asset-backed securities, as institutions sought to clean up their asset portfolios. On an annual basis, growth in the LCY bond market of the PRC decelerated to 14.1% y-o-y in Q4 2019 from 14.9% y-o-y in the prior quarter.

The next largest bond market in emerging East Asia was the Republic of Korea's, whose outstanding bonds totaled USD2,083.0 billion at the end of December. The Republic of Korea accounted for 13.0% of the region's aggregate bond stock at the end of the review period. Overall growth was clipped by a 0.2% q-o-q contraction in government bonds as the decline in the stock of central bank bonds exceeded the expansion in the stocks of central government bonds and other government bonds. In contrast, corporate bonds contributed to much of the growth in the Republic of Korea's LCY bond market, with growth picking up to 2.7% q-o-q in Q4 2019 from 2.3% q-o-q in Q3 2019. On an annual basis, the Republic of Korea's bond market growth accelerated to 7.6% y-o-y in Q4 2019 from 6.6% y-o-y in Q3 2019.

Hong Kong, China's LCY bond market inched up to a size of USD290.8 billion at the end of December on a marginal 0.1% q-o-q hike in Q4 2019, reversing a 0.9% q-o-q decline in the preceding quarter.

Hong Kong, China's government bond market was one of the two government bond markets in the region that posted faster q-o-q growth in Q4 2019 than in Q3 2019, as growth quickened to 1.0% q-o-q from 0.5% q-o-q. The stocks of both Exchange Fund Bills and Hong Kong Special Administrative Region bonds increased in Q4 2019. On the other hand, the stock of Exchange Fund Notes continued to decline with issuances, which have been limited to the 2-year tenor, occurring only once per quarter. The stock of corporate bonds also continued to decline, but with growth contracting at a slower pace of 0.9% q-o-q in Q4 2019 versus 2.4% q-o-q in the previous quarter. On an annual basis, growth in the LCY bond market of Hong Kong, China fell to 1.8% y-o-y in Q4 2019 from 4.2% y-o-y in Q3 2019.

At the end of December, the aggregate LCY bonds outstanding of member economies of the Association of Southeast Asian Nations (ASEAN) reached USD1,571.8 billion, with its share of the regional total holding broadly steady at 9.8%.[5] Growth on a q-o-q basis moderated to 1.2% in Q4 2019 from 1.8% in Q3 2019. Similar trends were observed on a y-o-y basis, as overall growth slipped to 9.6% from 10.2% during the review period. The stock of government bonds was down to USD1,076.8 billion at the end of December from USD1,064.5 billion at the end of September. Corporate bonds outstanding tallied USD495.0 billion at the end of December and accounted for a 31.5% share of the ASEAN total. All ASEAN bond markets experienced slower q-o-q and y-o-y growth in Q4 2019 than in Q3 2019, except for Thailand on a q-o-q basis and Singapore and Viet Nam on a y-o-y basis. The LCY bond markets of Thailand, Malaysia, and Singapore remained the largest in ASEAN at the end of December.

The outstanding amount of LCY bonds in Thailand totaled USD445.6 billion at the end of December. It was the only ASEAN market that posted faster q-o-q growth in Q4 2019 than in Q3 2019. Overall growth of the LCY bond market in Thailand rebounded to 2.2% q-o-q from a 0.7% q-o-q decline in Q3 2019. Much of the growth was contributed by increases in the stock of government bonds and, to a lesser extent, central bank bonds and state-owned enterprise bonds. Similarly, corporate bond market growth quickened to 1.6% q-o-q in Q4 2019 from 0.2% q-o-q in Q3 2019. On a y-o-y basis, Thai LCY bond

---

[5] LCY bond statistics for ASEAN include the markets of Indonesia, Malaysia, the Philippines, Singapore, Thailand, and Viet Nam.

market growth slipped to 6.4% in Q4 2019 from 6.6% in Q3 2019.

In Malaysia, total LCY bonds outstanding reached USD363.1 billion at the end of December. Growth contracted 0.5% q-o-q in Q4 2019, reversing the 0.3% q-o-q gain in the preceding quarter. The contraction stemmed largely from a decline in the stock of government bonds, which fell 1.6% q-o-q. The stocks of both central government bonds and central bank bills posted declines during the review period on account of low issuance volume for Treasury bonds and a relatively higher volume of maturities of central bank bills during the quarter. On the other hand, corporate bonds grew 0.7% q-o-q in Q4 2019, rebounding from a 0.2% q-o-q contraction posted in Q3 2019. The q-o-q increase in issuance of corporate bonds in Q4 2019 buoyed growth. On a y-o-y basis, Malaysia's bond market growth ebbed to 6.0% from 8.3% during the review period. Malaysia remained the region's largest *sukuk* (Islamic bond) market, with *sukuk* accounting for a 63.1% share of the Malaysian LCY bond market.

Singapore's LCY bonds outstanding totaled USD339.6 billion at the end of December, with growth moderating to 2.6% q-o-q in Q4 2019 from 4.9% q-o-q in the previous quarter. Growth was largely buoyed by government bonds on account of an increase in the stock of Singapore Government Securities bills and bonds, which more than offset the decline in the stock of Monetary Authority of Singapore (MAS) bills. Corporate bonds also contributed to overall growth, albeit to a lesser extent, with the stock of corporate bonds rising 1.7% q-o-q in Q4 2019. On a y-o-y basis, Singapore LCY bond market growth climbed to 14.7% in Q4 2019 from 11.9% in Q3 2019.

In Indonesia, the LCY bond market expanded to a size of USD238.8 billion at the end of December. Overall growth moderated to 2.5% q-o-q in Q4 2019 from 5.2% q-o-q in Q3 2019 amid a slowdown in issuance of both government and corporate bonds during the quarter. Government bonds continued to drive much of the growth, even with a decline in issuance as the government met its issuance needs earlier than planned by following a frontloading policy and accepting higher-than-targeted amounts during scheduled auctions. The government also complemented its LCY bond issuance with foreign-currency (FCY)-denominated issuance, allowing it to tap a bigger and more diversified investor base. The stock of central bank bonds contracted in Q4 2019 due to a relatively higher volume of maturities than issuance as Bank Indonesia limited new issuance of Sertifikat Bank Indonesia to *sukuk*. The corporate bond segment also contributed to the growth despite posting slower growth of 1.7% q-o-q in Q4 2019 versus 4.9% q-o-q in the previous quarter. On an annual basis, growth in Indonesia's LCY bond market slid to 16.6% y-o-y in Q4 2019 from 16.8% y-o-y in Q3 2019.

The Philippines' LCY bonds outstanding leveled off at USD131.2 billion at the end of December. Overall growth further weakened in Q4 2019, posting a decline of 0.8% q-o-q in Q4 2019 after contracting 0.1% q-o-q in Q3 2019. A huge volume of Treasury bills and bonds matured in Q4 2019, reducing the stock of government bonds outstanding despite a hefty issuance volume during the quarter. The stock of corporate bonds rose 4.0% q-o-q in Q4 2019 amid strong issuance. Annual bond market growth in the Philippines retreated to 9.0% y-o-y in Q4 2019 from 15.7% y-o-y in the preceding quarter.

At the end of December, Viet Nam's LCY bond market remained the smallest in emerging East Asia with bonds outstanding of USD53.6 billion. Overall bond market growth contracted 3.9% q-o-q due mainly to a decline in government bonds outstanding, which were pulled down by the maturation of all outstanding central bank bills, which were largely short-term in nature. The weak q-o-q growth of government bonds was further exacerbated by a 4.9% q-o-q contraction in the corporate bond stock. On a y-o-y basis, growth in Viet Nam's LCY bond market rose 4.1% in Q4 2019, up from 3.0% in the prior quarter.

Emerging East Asia's LCY bond market remained dominated by government bonds in Q4 2019. The region's government bond stock reached USD9,805.2 billion and accounted for a 61.1% share of the region's bond total at the end of December (**Table 1**). Government bond market growth moderated to 1.7% q-o-q and 11.4% y-o-y in Q4 2019 from 3.0% q-o-q and 11.6% y-o-y in Q3 2019. Five out of the nine markets in the region posted positive q-o-q growth in government bonds in Q4 2019. Those that posted q-o-q contractions were the government bond markets of the Republic of Korea, Malaysia, the Philippines, and Viet Nam.

At the end of December, the LCY government bond markets of the PRC and the Republic of Korea were

Table 1: Size and Composition of Local Currency Bond Markets

	Q4 2018 Amount (USD billion)	Q4 2018 % share	Q3 2019 Amount (USD billion)	Q3 2019 % share	Q4 2019 Amount (USD billion)	Q4 2019 % share	Growth Rate (LCY-base %) Q4 2018 q-o-q	Growth Rate (LCY-base %) Q4 2018 y-o-y	Growth Rate (LCY-base %) Q4 2019 q-o-q	Growth Rate (LCY-base %) Q4 2019 y-o-y	Growth Rate (USD-base %) Q4 2018 q-o-q	Growth Rate (USD-base %) Q4 2018 y-o-y	Growth Rate (USD-base %) Q4 2019 q-o-q	Growth Rate (USD-base %) Q4 2019 y-o-y
China, People's Rep. of														
Total	10,725	100.0	11,459	100.0	12,090	100.0	3.4	14.6	2.8	14.1	3.3	8.5	5.5	12.7
Government	6,961	64.9	7,402	64.6	7,753	64.1	2.2	14.1	2.0	12.7	2.0	7.9	4.7	11.4
Corporate	3,763	35.1	4,057	35.4	4,337	35.9	5.9	15.7	4.1	16.7	5.7	9.5	6.9	15.2
Hong Kong, China														
Total	284	100.0	289	100.0	291	100.0	2.4	16.7	0.1	1.8	2.4	16.4	0.7	2.4
Government	149	52.5	149	51.7	152	52.2	1.2	1.3	1.0	1.2	1.2	1.1	1.6	1.7
Corporate	135	47.5	140	48.3	139	47.8	3.7	40.2	(0.9)	2.6	3.7	39.9	(0.3)	3.1
Indonesia														
Total	197	100.0	228	100.0	239	100.0	2.7	13.7	2.5	16.6	6.3	7.1	4.9	21.1
Government	169	85.5	197	86.5	207	86.6	3.5	15.0	2.6	18.1	7.1	8.3	5.1	22.6
Corporate	29	14.5	31	13.5	32	13.4	(1.7)	6.3	1.7	8.1	1.8	0.2	4.1	12.2
Korea, Rep. of														
Total	2,015	100.0	1,982	100.0	2,083	100.0	0.7	3.8	1.6	7.6	0.5	(0.2)	5.1	3.4
Government	823	40.8	797	40.2	824	39.5	(1.5)	3.5	(0.2)	4.2	(1.7)	(0.5)	3.3	0.1
Corporate	1,192	59.2	1,184	59.8	1,259	60.5	2.2	4.0	2.7	9.9	2.1	(0.04)	6.3	5.6
Malaysia														
Total	339	100.0	357	100.0	363	100.0	1.6	8.9	(0.5)	6.0	1.7	6.6	1.8	7.1
Government	179	52.7	188	52.6	189	52.1	1.9	9.8	(1.6)	4.7	2.0	7.5	0.7	5.8
Corporate	160	47.3	169	47.4	174	47.9	1.3	8.0	0.7	7.6	1.5	5.7	3.1	8.7
Philippines														
Total	116	100.0	129	100.0	131	100.0	5.3	11.4	(0.8)	9.0	8.2	5.6	1.5	13.1
Government	91	78.4	101	78.4	101	77.4	4.1	7.4	(2.1)	7.5	7.1	1.8	0.2	11.5
Corporate	25	21.6	28	21.6	30	22.6	9.7	28.9	4.0	14.5	12.8	22.3	6.5	18.8
Singapore														
Total	292	100.0	322	100.0	340	100.0	0.1	7.2	2.6	14.7	0.4	5.0	5.3	16.2
Government	179	61.3	200	62.2	212	62.5	1.5	10.2	3.1	16.9	1.8	8.0	5.9	18.4
Corporate	113	38.7	122	37.8	127	37.5	(2.1)	2.7	1.7	11.3	(1.8)	0.6	4.4	12.7
Thailand														
Total	385	100.0	423	100.0	446	100.0	2.5	10.3	2.2	6.4	25.7	38.5	5.3	15.7
Government	278	72.2	301	71.2	318	71.4	3.3	9.6	2.5	5.2	23.0	33.6	5.6	14.5
Corporate	107	27.8	122	28.8	127	28.6	0.5	12.2	1.6	9.4	33.4	53.2	4.7	19.1
Viet Nam														
Total	51	100.0	56	100.0	54	100.0	(4.9)	10.4	(3.9)	4.1	(4.4)	8.1	(3.8)	4.1
Government	47	90.8	51	91.9	49	91.9	(6.1)	7.9	(3.9)	5.4	(5.6)	5.7	(3.7)	5.4
Corporate	5	9.2	5	8.1	4	8.1	8.8	43.1	(4.9)	(8.9)	9.4	40.2	(4.8)	(8.9)
Emerging East Asia														
Total	14,405	100.0	15,244	100.0	16,036	100.0	2.9	12.6	2.4	12.5	3.3	7.8	5.2	11.3
Government	8,875	61.6	9,387	61.6	9,805	61.1	1.8	12.4	1.7	11.4	2.3	7.5	4.5	10.5
Corporate	5,529	38.4	5,857	38.4	6,231	38.9	4.6	13.0	3.5	14.3	5.0	8.1	6.4	12.7
Japan														
Total	10,684	100.0	10,963	100.0	10,966	100.0	0.8	1.8	0.5	1.6	4.5	4.6	0.02	2.6
Government	9,961	93.2	10,187	92.9	10,180	92.8	0.7	1.8	0.4	1.2	4.4	4.6	(0.1)	2.2
Corporate	723	6.8	776	7.1	786	7.2	1.4	1.7	1.8	7.7	5.1	4.5	1.3	8.7
Memo Item: India														
Total	1,466	100.0	1,623	100.0	1,569	100.0	1.5	13.1	(2.7)	9.5	5.4	3.6	(3.4)	7.0
Government	1,044	71.2	1,188	73.2	1,129	71.9	0.5	13.8	(4.3)	10.6	4.5	4.2	(5.0)	8.1
Corporate	423	28.8	436	26.8	441	28.1	3.9	11.4	1.8	6.7	7.9	2.0	1.1	4.2

( ) = negative, LCY = local currency, q-o-q = quarter-on-quarter, Q3 = third quarter, Q4 = fourth quarter, USD = United States dollar, y-o-y = year-on-year.

Notes:
1. For Singapore, corporate bonds outstanding are based on *AsianBondsOnline* estimates.
2. For Hong Kong, China, the data series for corporate bonds outstanding was revised starting in 2018 to include more short-term debt securities.
3. Corporate bonds include issues by financial institutions.
4. Bloomberg LP end-of-period LCY–USD rates are used.
5. For LCY base, emerging East Asia growth figures are based on 31 December 2019 currency exchange rates and do not include currency effects.
6. Emerging East Asia comprises the People's Republic of China; Hong Kong, China; Indonesia; the Republic of Korea; Malaysia; the Philippines; Singapore; Thailand; and Viet Nam.

Sources: People's Republic of China (CEIC); Hong Kong, China (Hong Kong Monetary Authority); Indonesia (Bank Indonesia; Directorate General of Budget Financing and Risk Management, Ministry of Finance; and Indonesia Stock Exchange); Republic of Korea (*EDAILY BondWeb* and The Bank of Korea); Malaysia (Bank Negara Malaysia); Philippines (Bureau of the Treasury and Bloomberg LP); Singapore (Monetary Authority of Singapore, Singapore Government Securities, and Bloomberg LP); Thailand (Bank of Thailand); Viet Nam (Bloomberg LP and Vietnam Bond Market Association); Japan (Japan Securities Dealers Association); and India (Securities and Exchange Board of India and Bloomberg LP).

the region's leaders in terms of size. Together, these two markets accounted for 87.5% of emerging East Asia's aggregate bond stock, while ASEAN economies accounted for 11.0% of the regional government bond total. Among ASEAN members, the largest government bond markets were in Thailand, Singapore, and Indonesia.

The region's LCY corporate bond stock stood at USD6,230.5 billion at the end of December, accounting for a 38.9% share of the region's total LCY bond stock. On a q-o-q basis, growth in corporate bonds inched up to 3.5% in Q4 2019 from 3.2% in Q3 2019; on a y-o-y basis, growth eased to 14.3% from 15.5%. Except for Hong Kong, China and Viet Nam, all emerging East Asian markets saw positive q-o-q gains in their respective corporate bond markets. The corporate bond markets of the PRC and the Republic of Korea accounted for a combined 89.8% share of emerging East Asia's corporate bond stock. The corporate bond markets of ASEAN member economies had a 7.9% share of the region's corporate bond total. Among ASEAN members, the largest corporate bond markets were in Malaysia, Thailand, and Singapore.

As a percentage of the region's gross domestic product (GDP), emerging East Asia's LCY bond market climbed to an 83.3% share at the end of December from 82.6% at the end of September (**Table 2**). The region's government bonds-to-GDP ratio held steady at 50.9% between Q3 2019 and Q4 2019, while the corporate bonds-to-GDP ratio inched up to 32.4% from 31.7%. The Republic of Korea (130.5%) and Malaysia (104.6%) had the hightest bonds-to-GDP ratios in the region.

Foreign Investor Holdings

Foreign investor holdings of LCY government bonds were largely stable in the Q4 2019.

Emerging East Asia's foreign investor holdings were stable in Q4 2019 in most markets for which data are available (**Figure 2**).

The PRC's foreign holdings' share showed steady growth in each quarter of 2019, as foreign investors continued to be attracted to the PRC's bond market amid the gradual opening up of its capital market to foreigners.

In contrast, the share of foreign holdings in the Philippine LCY bond market peaked in December 2018

Table 2: Size and Composition of Local Currency Bond Markets (% of GDP)

	Q4 2018	Q3 2019	Q4 2019
China, People's Rep. of			
Total	80.2	84.3	85.0
Government	52.1	54.5	54.5
Corporate	28.2	29.8	30.5
Hong Kong, China			
Total	78.3	78.4	79.0
Government	41.1	40.5	41.2
Corporate	37.2	37.9	37.8
Indonesia			
Total	19.1	20.7	20.9
Government	16.4	17.9	18.1
Corporate	2.8	2.8	2.8
Korea, Rep. of			
Total	123.8	129.3	130.5
Government	50.6	52.0	51.6
Corporate	73.3	77.3	78.9
Malaysia			
Total	102.9	106.1	104.6
Government	54.3	55.8	54.4
Corporate	48.6	50.3	50.1
Philippines			
Total	35.0	36.7	35.7
Government	27.4	28.7	27.6
Corporate	7.5	7.9	8.1
Singapore			
Total	79.1	87.3	90.1
Government	48.6	54.3	56.3
Corporate	30.6	33.0	33.8
Thailand			
Total	76.0	77.1	78.4
Government	54.9	54.9	56.0
Corporate	21.1	22.2	22.4
Viet Nam			
Total	21.5	22.0	20.6
Government	19.5	20.2	18.9
Corporate	2.0	1.8	1.7
Emerging East Asia			
Total	79.3	82.6	83.3
Government	48.9	50.9	50.9
Corporate	30.4	31.7	32.4
Japan			
Total	214.2	214.2	214.8
Government	199.7	199.0	199.4
Corporate	14.5	15.2	15.4

GDP = gross domestic product, Q3 = third quarter, Q4 = fourth quarter.
Notes:
1. Data for GDP are from CEIC.
2. For Singapore, corporate bonds outstanding are based on *AsianBondsOnline* estimates.
3. For Hong Kong, China, the data series for corporate bonds outstanding was revised starting in 2018 to include more short-term debt securities.
Sources: People's Republic of China (CEIC); Hong Kong, China (Hong Kong Monetary Authority); Indonesia (Bank Indonesia; Directorate General of Budget Financing and Risk Management, Ministry of Finance; and Indonesia Stock Exchange); Republic of Korea (*EDAILY BondWeb* and The Bank of Korea); Malaysia (Bank Negara Malaysia); Philippines (Bureau of the Treasury and Bloomberg LP); Singapore (Monetary Authority of Singapore, Singapore Government Securities, and Bloomberg LP); Thailand (Bank of Thailand); Viet Nam (Bloomberg LP and Vietnam Bond Market Association); and Japan (Japan Securities Dealers Association).

Figure 2: Foreign Holdings of Local Currency Government Bonds in Select Asian Economies (% of total)

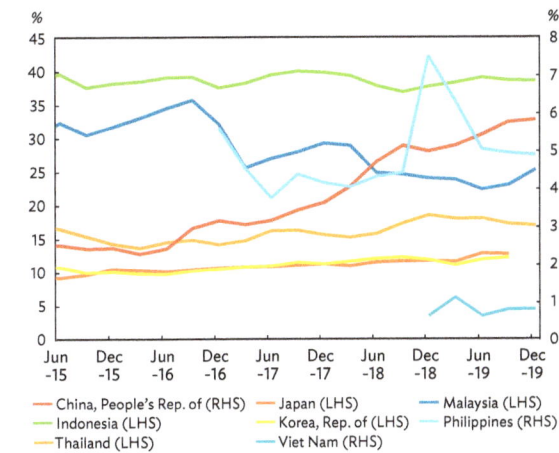

LHS = left-hand side, RHS = right-hand side.
Note: Data as of 31 December 2019 except for Japan and the Republic of Korea (30 September 2019).
Source: *AsianBondsOnline.*

Figure 3: Foreign Bond Flows in Select Emerging East Asian Economies

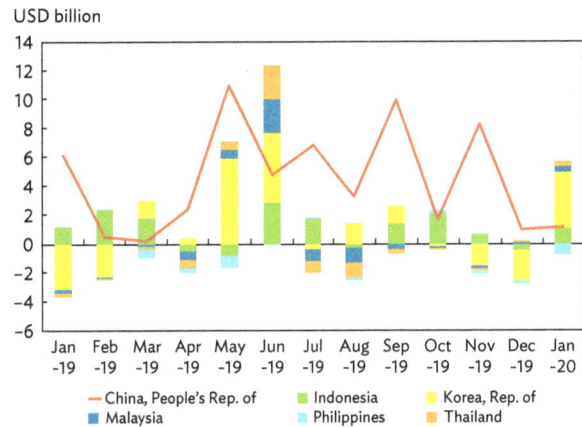

USD = United States dollar.
Notes:
1. The Republic of Korea and Thailand provided data on bond flows. For the People's Republic of China, Indonesia, Malaysia, and the Philippines, month-on-month changes in foreign holdings of local currency government bonds were used as a proxy for bond flows.
2. Data as of 31 January 2020.
3. Figures were computed based on 31 January 2020 exchange rates to avoid currency effects.
Sources: People's Republic of China (*Wind Information*); Indonesia (Directorate General of Budget Financing and Risk Management, Ministry of Finance); Republic of Korea (Financial Supervisory Service); Malaysia (Bank Negara Malaysia); Philippines (Bureau of the Treasury); and Thailand (Thai Bond Market Association).

and has since been on a downward trend despite a series of policy rate cuts by the Bangko Sentral ng Pilipinas (BSP) in 2019. Foreign investors took profits and reduced their holdings on expectations that inflation would trend upward again.

In Malaysia, there was a significant spike in the foreign holdings' share to 25.3% at the end of December from 23.0% at the end of September on the back of improved investor confidence as the government assured market participants that it would reach its budget deficit target of 3.4% of GDP for 2019, down from 3.7% in 2018.

In Indonesia, the share of foreign holdings was largely stable in Q4 2019, dipping marginally to 38.57% at the end of December from 38.64% at the end of September. In the Republic of Korea, the foreign holdings' share increased to 12.2% at the end of September from 11.9% at the end of June.

Foreign Bond Flows

Improved investor sentiment led to net bond inflows in January in all markets in the region except for the Philippines.

Trends in foreign bond flows were similar in Q4 2019 to the previous quarter for all economies in the region for which data are available except the Republic of Korea.

The PRC, Indonesia, and Malaysia recorded foreign bond inflows in Q4 2019, while the Republic of Korea, the Philippines, and Thailand posted outflows (**Figure 3**).

In the PRC, the LCY bond market continued to attract foreign investors, with total inflows reaching USD11.0 billion in Q4 2019, although this was lower than inflows in Q3 2019 of USD20.2 billion.

In Indonesia, foreign bond flows into the government bond market declined to USD2.4 billion in Q4 2019 from USD3.0 billion in Q3 2019. In Malaysia, strong inflows were recorded in November and December, leading to net inflows of USD3.5 billion in Q4 2019 versus USD1.6 billion in Q3 2019, as investor confidence improved on the government's strengthened finances.

The Philippines and Thailand experienced roughly similar net outflows in Q4 2019 of USD0.2 billion each. In the Philippines, the outflows were mostly related to investors taking profits. In Thailand, the outflows were largely related to political uncertainty over the delayed passage of the government's budget.

The Republic of Korea was the only market to post outflows in each month of Q4 2019, leading to net outflows of USD3.7 billion, reversing the previous quarter's USD2.3 billion inflows, largely due to profit-taking.

News of the Phase 1 trade deal between the PRC and the United States (US), which was signed on 18 January, helped lift investor sentiment. Except for the Philippines, all markets in the region reported net bond inflows in January.

LCY Bond Issuance

Emerging East Asia's aggregate LCY bond issuance fell 9.5% q-o-q to USD1.4 trillion in Q4 2019, dragged down by lower debt sales in the PRC and weak issuance growth in the majority of the region.

Emerging East Asia's total LCY bond issuance declined 9.5% q-o-q to USD1,438.4 billion in Q4 2019 (**Table 3**). The contraction followed tepid 0.7% q-o-q growth in the previous quarter. Total government bond issuance in the region dropped 20.5% q-o-q, offsetting the modest 4.9% q-o-q growth in corporate debt issuance. The region's largest bond market in the PRC experienced a sharp decline in issuance of 17.2% q-o-q. Indonesia (–15.2%); Thailand (–2.1%); Hong Kong, China (–2.0%); and Malaysia (–1.2%) also registered q-o-q contractions in debt sales. The Republic of Korea, which is home to the region's second-largest bond market, posted strong issuance growth of 15.3% q-o-q. The Philippines, Singapore, and Viet Nam showed modest issuance growth of 8.8% q-o-q, 2.8% q-o-q, and 1.1% q-o-q, respectively. The contractions in issuance in five out of the region's nine economies, particularly the PRC and Indonesia, offset relatively weak issuance growth in the rest of emerging East Asia. On an annual basis, total LCY issuance rose 12.5% y-o-y, buoyed by strong growth in both the government and corporate segments. With the exception of Malaysia, all markets registered positive y-o-y growth in Q4 2019.

The region's total LCY bond issuance in the government sector dropped to USD715.7 billion in Q4 2019. The 20.5% q-o-q contraction in Q4 2019 followed a 5.8% q-o-q drop in Q3 2019, as most governments tapered their frontloading issuance policies during the

last half of the year. The PRC posted a 38.0% q-o-q contraction in government borrowing in Q4 2019 as many local governments had met their issuance targets in the previous quarter. Indonesia, the Republic of Korea, Malaysia, the Philippines, and Thailand also registered declines in government bond issuance in Q4 2019. Only Hong Kong, China; Singapore; and Viet Nam posted modest gains in government debt issuance during the quarter, with Singapore showing the largest increase in government bond sales at 4.5% q-o-q.

Central bank bond issuance in emerging East Asia rose 1.6% q-o-q in Q4 2019, while Treasury and other government bond issuance contracted sharply by 33.0% q-o-q. Government bonds comprised 49.8% of total issuance in emerging East Asia in Q4 2019, down from 56.7% in Q3 2019. On an annual basis, the region's government debt issuance rose 9.1% y-o-y in Q4 2019.

The region's LCY corporate debt issuance continued its uptrend in Q4 2019, albeit at a slower pace than in Q3 2019. Total corporate bond issuance in Q4 2019 reached USD722.7 billion, rising 4.9% q-o-q following a 10.7% q-o-q expansion in the previous quarter. The Republic of Korea, the second-largest bond market in the region, saw a 30.5% q-o-q increase in corporate debt sales following the Bank of Korea's policy rate reduction in October. Similarly, corporate bond issuance in the Philippines surged 42.4% q-o-q in Q4 2019 as companies took advantage of low borrowing costs. The PRC and Malaysia recorded muted growth in corporate debt sales in Q4 2019 at 1.7% and 2.6% q-o-q, respectively. Hong Kong, China; Indonesia; Singapore; Thailand; and Viet Nam saw contractions in corporate debt during the quarter. On an annual basis, the region's LCY corporate debt issuance rose 16.2% y-o-y in Q4 2019, down from the robust 31.8% y-o-y growth posted in the previous quarter.

The PRC's LCY bond issuance in Q4 2019 fell 17.2% q-o-q to USD833.6 billion, dragged down by a 38.0% q-o-q contraction in government debt sales that offset the weak 1.7% q-o-q growth in corporate debt issuance. The decline in the government bonds segment was mostly driven by reduced issuance of local government bonds intended for infrastructure financing to help boost economic growth. Local governments were required to complete nearly all of their bond issuance quotas by September, and allocate proceeds by October, resulting in reduced issuance

Table 3: Local-Currency–Denominated Bond Issuance (gross)

	Q4 2018		Q3 2019		Q4 2019		Growth Rate (LCY-base %)		Growth Rate (USD-base %)	
	Amount (USD billion)	% share	Amount (USD billion)	% share	Amount (USD billion)	% share	Q4 2019		Q4 2019	
							q-o-q	y-o-y	q-o-q	y-o-y
China, People's Rep. of										
Total	760	100.0	981	100.0	834	100.0	(17.2)	11.1	(15.0)	9.7
Government	299	39.4	467	47.6	297	35.7	(38.0)	0.7	(36.3)	(0.6)
Central Bank	0	0.0	0	0.0	0	0.0	–	–	–	–
Treasury and Other Govt.	299	39.4	467	47.6	297	35.7	(38.0)	0.7	(36.3)	(0.6)
Corporate	461	60.6	514	52.4	536	64.3	1.7	17.9	4.4	16.4
Hong Kong, China										
Total	126	100.0	130	100.0	128	100.0	(2.0)	1.3	(1.4)	1.8
Government	106	84.4	107	82.1	109	85.2	1.7	2.3	2.3	2.8
Central Bank	105	83.4	106	81.8	109	84.6	1.4	2.7	2.0	3.2
Treasury and Other Govt.	1	1.0	0.5	0.4	0.8	0.6	71.1	(31.6)	72.1	(31.2)
Corporate	20	15.6	23	17.9	19	14.8	(18.9)	(4.2)	(18.4)	(3.7)
Indonesia										
Total	11	100.0	24	100.0	21	100.0	(15.2)	87.5	(13.2)	94.6
Government	10	91.3	21	87.2	19	88.3	(14.1)	81.4	(12.1)	88.3
Central Bank	2	15.4	8	33.5	8	44.3	(1.0)	375.4	1.3	393.4
Treasury and Other Govt.	8	75.9	13	53.7	10	49.2	(22.3)	21.5	(20.5)	26.1
Corporate	0.9	8.7	3	12.8	2	11.7	(22.6)	151.8	(20.8)	161.4
Korea, Rep. of										
Total	182	100.0	164	100.0	196	100.0	15.3	12.1	19.3	7.7
Government	60	32.9	63	38.6	60	30.5	(9.0)	3.9	(5.8)	(0.2)
Central Bank	33	17.9	30	18.3	29	14.6	(8.1)	(8.5)	(4.9)	(12.0)
Treasury and Other Govt.	27	15.0	33	20.3	31	15.9	(9.8)	18.6	(6.6)	14.0
Corporate	122	67.1	101	61.4	136	69.5	30.5	16.1	35.1	11.6
Malaysia										
Total	25	100.0	20	100.0	20	100.0	(1.2)	(18.2)	1.2	(17.4)
Government	14	57.7	9	45.6	9	43.5	(5.7)	(38.3)	(3.5)	(37.7)
Central Bank	7	30.0	2	10.2	3	14.6	41.9	(60.3)	45.2	(59.8)
Treasury and Other Govt.	7	27.7	7	35.4	6	28.9	(19.3)	(14.5)	(17.4)	(13.6)
Corporate	10	42.3	11	54.4	12	56.5	2.6	9.2	5.0	10.3
Philippines										
Total	7	100.0	7	100.0	7	100.0	8.8	0.1	11.3	3.9
Government	5	65.4	5	78.5	5	71.9	(0.4)	10.1	1.9	14.2
Central Bank	0	0.0	0	0.0	0	0.0	–	–	–	–
Treasury and Other Govt.	5	65.4	5	78.5	5	71.9	(0.4)	10.1	1.9	14.2
Corporate	2	34.6	1	21.5	2	28.1	42.4	(18.7)	45.8	(15.6)
Singapore										
Total	100	100.0	124	100.0	130	100.0	2.8	28.2	5.6	29.8
Government	97	96.9	120	96.8	128	98.4	4.5	30.2	7.3	31.9
Central Bank	94	93.2	94	75.9	103	79.3	7.6	9.2	10.4	10.5
Treasury and Other Govt.	4	3.7	26	21.0	25	19.1	(6.4)	556.9	(3.9)	565.2
Corporate	3	3.1	4	3.2	2	1.6	(48.9)	(34.6)	(47.6)	(33.8)
Thailand										
Total	70	100.0	78	100.0	79	100.0	(2.1)	3.2	0.9	12.3
Government	59	84.3	65	82.8	66	83.7	(0.9)	2.5	2.1	11.6
Central Bank	53	75.7	59	75.7	59	74.8	(3.3)	2.0	(0.4)	11.0
Treasury and Other Govt.	6	8.6	5	7.0	7	8.9	24.3	7.2	28.1	16.6
Corporate	11	15.7	13	17.2	13	16.3	(7.6)	7.0	(4.8)	16.4

continued on next page

Table 3 *continued*

	Q4 2018		Q3 2019		Q4 2019		Growth Rate (LCY-base %)		Growth Rate (USD-base %)	
	Amount (USD billion)	% share	Amount (USD billion)	% share	Amount (USD billion)	% share	Q4 2019		Q4 2019	
							q-o-q	y-o-y	q-o-q	y-o-y
Viet Nam										
Total	4	100.0	22	100.0	22	100.0	1.1	440.6	1.3	440.6
Government	4	86.8	22	99.4	22	99.7	1.4	520.8	1.5	520.9
Central Bank	0.7	16.1	19	89.7	20	88.9	0.2	2879.4	0.3	2879.7
Treasury and Other Govt.	3	70.7	2	9.7	2	10.8	12.4	(17.3)	12.6	(17.3)
Corporate	0.5	13.2	0.1	0.6	0	0.3	(44.8)	(86.3)	(44.7)	(86.2)
Emerging East Asia										
Total	1,285	100.0	1,550	100.0	1,438	100.0	(9.5)	12.5	(7.2)	11.9
Government	654	50.9	879	56.7	716	49.8	(20.5)	9.1	(18.6)	9.4
Central Bank	294	22.9	319	20.6	330	23.0	1.6	10.3	3.6	12.3
Treasury and Other Govt.	360	28.0	560	36.1	385	26.8	(33.0)	8.1	(31.2)	7.0
Corporate	631	49.1	671	43.3	723	50.2	4.9	16.2	7.7	14.5
Japan										
Total	417	100.0	389	100.0	373	100.0	(3.6)	(11.3)	(4.0)	(10.4)
Government	382	91.7	357	91.9	356	95.4	0.1	(7.7)	(0.4)	(6.8)
Central Bank	15	3.5	0	0.0	0	0.0	–	(100.0)	–	(100.0)
Treasury and Other Govt.	367	88.2	357	91.9	356	95.4	0.1	(4.1)	(0.4)	(3.1)
Corporate	35	8.3	31	8.1	17	4.6	(44.8)	(50.6)	(45.0)	(50.1)

( ) = negative, – = not applicable, LCY = local currency, q-o-q = quarter-on-quarter, Q3 = third quarter, Q4 = fourth quarter, USD = United States dollar, y-o-y = year-on-year.
Notes:
1. Corporate bonds include issues by financial institutions.
2. For Hong Kong, China, the data series for corporate bond issuance was revised starting in 2018 to include more short-term debt securities.
3. Bloomberg LP end-of-period LCY–USD rates are used.
4. For LCY base, emerging East Asia growth figures are based on 31 December 2019 currency exchange rates and do not include currency effects.
Sources: People's Republic of China (CEIC); Hong Kong, China (Hong Kong Monetary Authority); Indonesia (Bank Indonesia; Directorate General of Budget Financing and Risk Management, Ministry of Finance; and Indonesia Stock Exchange); Republic of Korea (*EDAILY BondWeb* and The Bank of Korea); Malaysia (Bank Negara Malaysia); Philippines (Bloomberg LP); Singapore (Singapore Government Securities and Bloomberg LP); Thailand (Bank of Thailand and ThaiBMA); Viet Nam (Bloomberg LP and Vietnam Bond Market Association); and Japan (Japan Securities Dealers Association).

in Q4 2019. Government bonds comprised 35.7% of total issuance in the PRC during the quarter. Corporate issuance in Q4 2019 amounted to USD536.3 billion, registering a modest 4.9% rise from the previous quarter. Despite the decline in total bond issuance during the quarter, the PRC remained the region's largest issuer, accounting for 58.0% of emerging East Asia's total LCY bond issuance in Q4 2019.

The Republic of Korea's LCY bond issuance rose 15.3% q-o-q to reach USD196.1 billion in Q4 2019. The growth in the Republic of Korea's debt issuance helped offset weak issuance in other economies in the region. With 13.6% of the region's total issuance, the Republic of Korea remained the second-most active bond market in emerging East Asia in terms of issuance. Government issuance totaled USD59.8 billion, down 9.0% q-o-q in Q4 2019 following a 6.6% decline in the previous quarter. Declining issuance in the second half of the year resulted from the frontloading of government debt

sales in the first half. Central bank issuance contracted 8.1% q-o-q in Q4 2019, while Treasury and other bond issuance dropped 9.8% q-o-q. Strong corporate debt sales, which surged 30.5% q-o-q, offset the weak growth in the government bond sector. Taking advantage of low borrowing costs after the Bank of Korea lowered its policy rate to 1.25% in October, corporates issued a total of USD136.3 billion in Q4 2019. The Republic of Korea's corporate bond issuance accounted for 18.9% of the regional total in Q4 2019.

Hong Kong, China's LCY bond issuance contracted 2.0% in Q4 2019, the same pace of contraction posted in the previous quarter. Government bond issuance amounted to USD109.5 billion, with growth rising slightly to 1.7% q-o-q in Q4 2019 from the previous quarter's modest 0.5% q-o-q gain. Issuance of Exchange Fund Bills and Notes by the Hong Kong Monetary Authority rose 1.4% q-o-q, while issuance of Hong Kong Special Administrative Region bonds expanded 71.1% q-o-q as the government issued 3-year and 5-year bonds in October and November. Corporate bond sales continued to decline in Q4 2019, falling 18.9% q-o-q after a 12.1% q-o-q drop in Q3 2019. Months of prolonged political protests and the ensuing economic recession curtailed appetite for corporate borrowing during the quarter.

ASEAN member economies issued a total of USD280.2 billion of LCY bonds in Q4 2019, accounting for 19.5% of the region's total issuance. Singapore remained the largest issuer of LCY bond debt within ASEAN, while the Philippines was the smallest issuer during the quarter. Half of ASEAN markets—the Philippines, Singapore, and Viet Nam— experienced a q-o-q expansion in issuance, while the other half— Indonesia, Malaysia, and Thailand—saw declines in issuance during the quarter. ASEAN economies' total government debt issuance amounted to USD249.2 billion, comprising 88.9% of their total issuance. Corporate debt issuance comprised the remaining 11.1%, amounting to USD31.1 billion.

In Indonesia, LCY bond issuance dropped 15.2% q-o-q in Q4 2019 following 45.0% q-o-q growth in the previous quarter. Total issuance during the quarter amounted to USD21.1 billion, comprising USD18.7 billion in government bonds and USD2.5 billion in corporate debt. Government bond issuance dropped 14.1% q-o-q, reversing the 43.8% q-o-q rise in the preceding quarter. The reduced issuance in Q4 2019 was due to the government's completion of its financing plans ahead of schedule, resulting in the cancelation of auctions previously scheduled in December. Corporate bond issuance was also less active in Q4 2019, declining 22.6% q-o-q. Issuance in the corporate sector comprised 11.7% of total issuance in Q4 2019, slightly down from 12.8% in the previous quarter.

Malaysia's LCY bond issuance dipped 1.2% q-o-q to USD20.4 billion in Q4 2019, recovering from a 25.2% q-o-q contraction posted in Q3 2019. Government bond issuance dropped 5.7% q-o-q during the quarter. While central bank issuance expanded 41.9% q-o-q, the growth was partly offset by a 19.3% q-o-q fall in Treasury and other government bond issuance. The government tapered its bond issuance during the quarter, with the smallest amount of bond issuance in December. Corporate bond issuance posted 2.6% q-o-q growth in Q4 2019, recovering from a 36.0% q-o-q drop in the previous quarter.

In the Philippines, total bond issuance rose 8.8% q-o-q to USD7.5 billion in Q4 2019. The growth was driven by strong corporate bond issuance, which surged 42.4% q-o-q during the quarter. Meanwhile, government bond issuance dipped 0.4% q-o-q as the Bureau of the Treasury had already met its annual issuance target during the preceding 3 quarters. Reduced government bond issuance was also partly due to lower spending in the first half of 2019 as a result of the late approval of the government's budget. In contrast, corporate debt sales amounted to USD2.1 billion in Q4 2019. Firms took advantage of low borrowing costs after the BSP lowered its policy rate to 4.00% in September, the third policy rate cut of the year.

Singapore's total LCY bond issuance amounted to USD130.4 billion in Q4 2019 on growth of 2.8% q-o-q and 28.2% y-o-y. Issuance during the quarter was dominated by government bonds, particularly MAS bills, which rose 7.6% q-o-q to USD103.5 billion. The 6.4% q-o-q drop in the issuance of Singapore Government Securities bills and bonds partly offset issuance growth for MAS bills. Issuance of corporate debt was less active in Q4 2019, amounting to USD2.1 billion, which was about half of the level of issuance in the previous quarter.

In Thailand, total LCY bond issuance fell 2.1% q-o-q to USD78.8 billion in Q4 2019, due to contractions in both government and corporate debt issuance. Government bond issuance showed a marginal decline of 0.9% q-o-q, driven by a 3.3% q-o-q drop in Bank of Thailand bond sales, which offset the 24.3% q-o-q growth in Treasury and other bond issuance. Q4 2019 saw a rise in issuance of long-dated government bonds, as the government issued two 30-year tenors and one 48-year tenor. Corporate bond issuance declined 7.6% q-o-q in Q4 2019, reflecting a slight recovery from the 20.9% q-o-q contraction in issuance posted in Q3 2019. The Bank of Thailand lowered its policy rate to 1.25% in November, the second policy rate reduction of the year. Low borrowing costs gave rise to the issuance of several perpetual corporate bonds during the quarter: Indorama Ventures, Thai Union Group, Bangchak, and B Grimm Power issued a total of USD1.3 billion of perpetual bonds in Q4 2019.

Viet Nam's total bond issuance rose 1.1% q-o-q to USD21.9 billion in Q4 2019, recovering from an 8.1% q-o-q drop in the previous quarter. Government bond issuance rose 1.4% q-o-q, driven by issuance of government-guaranteed bonds. Central bank bond issuance in Q4 2019 was roughly at par with the previous quarter, while the issuance of Treasury and other bonds rose 12.4% q-o-q. Viet Nam's bond issuance consisted almost entirely of government bonds, which comprised a 99.7% share of total bond issuance in Q4 2019. Corporate bond issuance amounted to USD0.1 billion, falling 44.8% q-o-q in Q4 2019. At only 0.3%, the corporate segment's share of total bond issuance in Viet Nam was the lowest in the region.

Cross-Border Bond Issuance

Intraregional bond issuance in emerging East Asia totaled USD2.2 billion in Q4 2019.

Emerging East Asia's total intraregional bond issuance reached USD2.2 billion in Q4 2019, declining 33.8% q-o-q from the USD3.3 billion raised in Q3 2019 and 59.5% y-o-y from Q4 2018. Institutions from only four economies issued cross-border bonds in Q4 2019, down from six economies in Q3 2019. The slowdown in cross-border issuance may be attributed to the growth slowdown in most economies in the region, particularly in the PRC, which lessened demand for capital expenditure funding and borrowing requirements. The PRC continued to dominate the cross-border market as it accounted for 62.0% of the regional aggregate (**Figure 4**). The Republic of Korea

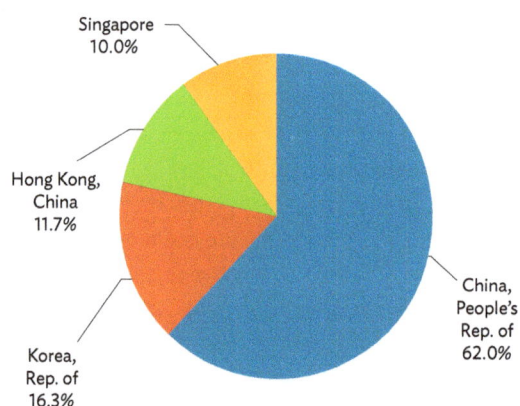

Figure 4: Origin Economies of Intra-Emerging East Asian Bond Issuance in the Fourth Quarter of 2019

Source: *AsianBondsOnline* calculations based on Bloomberg LP data.

followed next accounting for a regional share of 16.3%. Other economies that issued cross-border bonds were Hong Kong, China and Singapore.

Cross-border bond issuance in the PRC declined in Q4 2019 to USD1.4 billion, down 42.4% q-o-q from USD2.4 billion in Q3 2019. Half of the region's 18 cross-border bond issuers during the quarter were from the PRC. This includes government-owned China Development Bank, which remained the top issuer, raising USD590.4 million worth of bonds denominated in Hong Kong dollars. The second-largest cross-border issuer was China Yuhua, which issued USD268.0 million of 5-year Hong Kong dollar bonds. Eastern Air, the third-largest cross-border issuer in the region, raised USD259.5 million worth of 3-year bonds denominated in Korean won. The remaining six companies that issued cross-border bonds from the PRC raised an aggregate USD232.1 million worth of bonds denominated in Hong Kong dollars and Malaysian ringgit.

In Q4 2019, the Republic of Korea surpassed Hong Kong, China as the economy with the second-largest volume of cross-border bond issuances. Four institutions raised funds totaling USD357.7 million. The Export–Import Bank of Korea raised USD133.4 million via issuance of 5-year and 1-year bonds denominated in Indonesian rupiah and Hong Kong dollars. State-owned Korea Development Bank issued USD81.2 million worth of 5-year bonds. Other companies that issued cross-border bonds were POSCO International (USD126.3 million) and Woori Bank (USD16.7 million).

In Hong Kong, China, cross-border bond issuances declined by more than half to USD257.2 million in Q4 2019 from USD590.6 million in the previous quarter. The companies that issued cross-border bonds in Q4 2019 were Hebei New Co-Op International (USD114.9 million), Hong Kong Land Treasury (USD111.4 million), and KGI International (USD30.9 million). Cross-border bonds issued in Hong Kong, China were denominated in Chinese yuan and Singapore dollars.

Only two companies in Singapore issued cross-border bonds, with the total funds raised reaching USD219.9 million, all of which was denominated in Chinese yuan. China Construction Bank Singapore issued USD143.6 million of 2-year bonds, while Nomura

International Funding issued USD76.3 million worth of bonds with tenors of 9.5 years and 10 years.

The top 10 issuers in the region had an aggregate issuance volume of USD2.0 billion and comprised 89.0% of the regional total for the quarter. Five of the leading issuers were from the PRC, issuing bonds denominated in Hong Kong dollars, Korean won, and Singapore dollars. Three were from the Republic of Korea; the remaining two were from Hong Kong, China and Singapore. The top three issuers were from the PRC: China Development Bank, China Yuhua, and Eastern Air.

The Hong Kong dollar remained the predominant currency of cross-border bond issuance in Q4 2019 with an aggregate volume of USD1.2 billion, which comprised 56.0% of the regional total (**Figure 5**). Firms from the PRC and the Republic of Korea issued bonds denominated in Hong Kong dollars. The second-most widely used currency was the Chinese yuan with total cross-border issuance from firms in Hong Kong, China and Singapore reaching USD365.7 million and comprising a regional share of 16.6% of the total. Other currencies include the Korean won (11.8%, USD259.6 million); Singapore dollar (10.8%, USD237.8 million); Indonesian rupiah (4.6%, USD101.3 million); and Malaysian ringgit (0.2%, USD4.0 million).

G3 Currency Bond Issuance

Total G3 currency bond issuance in emerging East Asia amounted to USD346.6 billion in 2019.

G3 currency bonds issued in emerging East Asia in 2019 totaled USD346.6 billion, an increase of 17.9% y-o-y from USD294.0 billion in 2018 (**Table 4**).[6,7] The growth was driven by increased G3 issuance in all economies in emerging East Asia except Cambodia, Indonesia, the Republic of Korea, and Singapore.

During the review period, 91.3% of all G3 currency bonds issued were denominated in US dollars, 6.4% were in euros, and 2.2% were in Japanese yen. In 2019, a total of USD316.6 billion worth of bonds denominated in US dollars were issued in emerging East Asia, representing an increase of 19.6% y-o-y. The equivalent of USD22.2 billion of EUR-denominated bonds were issued during the review period, a decline of 3.8% y-o-y. Bonds issued in Japanese yen totaled USD7.8 billion, an increase of 23.7% y-o-y, spurred by Malaysia's samurai bond issuance in March.

The PRC continued to dominate all economies in the issuance of G3 currency bonds, totaling USD225.2 billion in 2019, which mainly comprised issuance in US dollars. This was followed by Hong Kong, China with USD31.9 billion and the Republic of Korea with USD29.4 billion, both issuing mainly in US dollars as well.

In 2019, G3 currency bond issuance increased on a y-o-y basis in Malaysia (371.3%); Hong Kong, China (45.8%); Viet Nam (41.8%); the PRC (22.6%); Thailand (9.8%); and the Philippines (9.6%). Issuance of G3 currency bonds in 2019 declined on a y-o-y basis in Singapore (−39.8%), Indonesia (−14.1%), and the Republic of Korea (−3.3%). The Lao People's Democratic Republic issued G3 currency bonds in 2019 but not in 2018. On the other hand, Cambodia issued G3 currency bonds in 2018 but not in 2019.

The PRC accounted for 65.0% of all G3 currency issuance in emerging East Asia in 2019, issuing USD211.8 billion in US dollars, the equivalent of USD13.2 billion in euros,

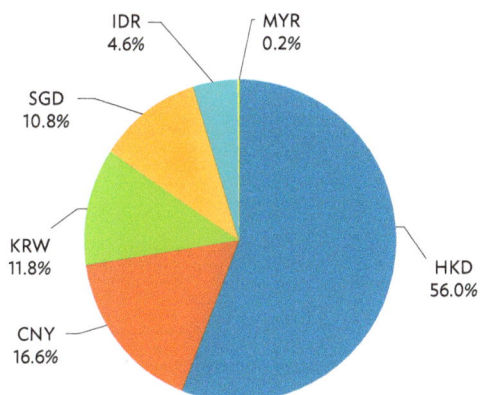

Figure 5: Currency Shares of Intra-Emerging East Asian Bond Issuance in the Fourth Quarter of 2019

CNY = Chinese yuan, HKD = Hong Kong dollar, IDR = Indonesian rupiah, KRW = Korean won, MYR = Malaysian ringgit, SGD = Singapore dollar.
Source: *AsianBondsOnline* calculations based on Bloomberg LP data.

---

6 For the discussion on G3 issuance, emerging East Asia comprises Cambodia; the People's Republic of China; Hong Kong, China; Indonesia; the Republic of Korea; the Lao People's Democratic Republic; Malaysia; the Philippines; Singapore; Thailand; and Viet Nam.
7 G3 currency bonds are denominated in either euros, Japanese yen, or US dollars.

Table 4: G3 Currency Bond Issuance

2018			2019		
Issuer	Amount (USD billion)	Issue Date	Issuer	Amount (USD billion)	Issue Date
Cambodia	**0.3**		**Cambodia**	**0.0**	
China, People's Rep. of	**183.6**		**China, People's Rep. of**	**225.2**	
Tencent Holdings 3.595% 2028	2.5	19-Jan-18	Tencent Holdings 3.975% 2029	3.0	11-Apr-19
CNAC (HK) Finbridge Company 5.125% 2028	1.8	14-Mar-18	People's Republic of China (Sovereign) 0.125% 2026	2.2	12-Nov-19
Scenery Journey 11.000% 2020	1.6	6-Nov-18	People's Republic of China (Sovereign) 1.950% 2024	2.0	3-Dec-19
Others	177.8		Others	218.0	
Hong Kong, China	**21.9**		**Hong Kong, China**	**31.9**	
CHMT Peaceful Development Asia Property 7.5% 2019	3.3	25-Apr-18	Celestial Miles 5.75% Perpetual	1.0	31-Jan-19
Bank of China (Hong Kong) 5.9% Perpetual	3.0	14-Sep-18	Hong Kong, China (Sovereign) 2.50% 2024	1.0	28-May-19
ICBC (Asia) 4.9% Perpetual	2.5	21-Mar-18	AIA Group 3.60% 2029	1.0	9-Apr-19
Others	13.0		Others	28.9	
Indonesia	**26.1**		**Indonesia**	**22.4**	
Perusahaan Penerbit SBSN *Sukuk* 4.40% 2028	1.8	1-Mar-18	Perusahaan Penerbit SBSN *Sukuk* 4.45% 2029	1.3	20-Feb-19
Indonesia Asahan Aluminium 5.71% 2023	1.3	15-Nov-18	Indonesia (Sovereign) 1.40% 2031	1.1	30-Oct-19
Indonesia (Sovereign) 4.75% 2029	1.3	11-Dec-18	Indonesia (Sovereign) 3.70% 2049	1.0	30-Oct-19
Others	21.8		Others	19.0	
Korea, Rep. of	**30.4**		**Korea, Rep. of**	**29.4**	
Hanwha Life Insurance 4.700% 2048	1.0	23-Apr-18	Republic of Korea (Sovereign) 2.500% 2029	1.0	19-Jun-19
Korea Development Bank 0.625% 2023	0.9	17-Jul-18	Export–Import Bank of Korea 0.375% 2024	0.8	26-Mar-19
Export–Import Bank of Korea 0.625% 2023	0.9	11-Jul-18	LG Display 1.500% 2024	0.7	22-Aug-19
Others	27.6		Others	26.8	
Lao People's Democratic Rep.	**0.0**		**Lao People's Democratic Rep.**	**0.2**	
Malaysia	**2.9**		**Malaysia**	**13.7**	
TNB Global Ventures Capital 4.85100% 2028	0.8	1-Nov-18	Malaysia (Sovereign) 0.530% 2029	1.8	15-Mar-19
Maybank 3.51813% 2023	0.3	10-Aug-18	Resorts World Las Vegas 4.625% 2029	1.0	16-Apr-19
Others	1.9		Others	10.9	
Philippines	**6.2**		**Philippines**	**6.7**	
Philippines (Sovereign) 3.00% 2028	2.0	1-Feb-18	Philippines (Sovereign) 3.750% 2029	1.5	14-Jan-19
Philippines (Sovereign) 0.38% 2021	1.0	15-Aug-18	Philippines (Sovereign) 0.875% 2027	0.8	17-May-19
Others	3.2		Others	4.4	
Singapore	**16.1**		**Singapore**	**9.7**	
Temasek Financial 3.625% 2028	1.4	1-Aug-18	DBS Group 2.85% 2022	0.8	16-Apr-19
DBS Bank 3.300% 2021	1.3	27-Nov-18	BOC Aviation 3.50% 2024	0.8	10-Apr-19
Others	13.5		Others	8.2	
Thailand	**5.9**		**Thailand**	**6.4**	
Bangkok Bank/Hong Kong 4.45% 2028	0.6	19-Sep-18	Bangkok Bank/Hong Kong 3.733% 2034	1.2	25-Sep-19
Bangkok Bank/Hong Kong 4.05% 2024	0.6	19-Sep-18	Kasikornbank 3.343% 2031	0.8	2-Oct-19
Others	4.7		Others	4.4	
Viet Nam	**0.7**		**Viet Nam**	**1.0**	
Emerging East Asia Total	**294.0**		**Emerging East Asia Total**	**346.4**	
Memo Items:			**Memo Items:**		
India	**6.4**		**India**	**21.9**	
Export–Import Bank of India 3.875% 2028	1.0	1-Feb-18	Indian Oil Corporation 4.75% 2024	0.9	16-Jan-19
Others	5.4		Others	21.0	
Sri Lanka	**3.9**		**Sri Lanka**	**4.9**	
Sri Lanka (Sovereign) 5.75% 2023	1.3	18-Apr-18	Sri Lanka (Sovereign) 7.55% 2030	1.5	28-Jun-19
Others	2.7		Others	3.4	

USD = United States dollar.
Notes:
1. Data exclude certificates of deposits.
2. G3 currency bonds are bonds denominated in either euros, Japanese yen, or US dollars.
3. Bloomberg LP end-of-period rates are used.
4. Emerging East Asia comprises Cambodia; the People's Republic of China; Hong Kong, China; Indonesia; the Republic of Korea; the Lao People's Democratic Republic; Malaysia; the Philippines; Singapore; Thailand; and Viet Nam.
5. Figures after the issuer name reflect the coupon rate and year of maturity of the bond.
Source: *AsianBondsOnline* calculations based on Bloomberg LP data.

and the equivalent of USD0.2 billion in Japanese yen. In Q4 2019, the Government of the PRC issued three tranches of EUR-denominated bonds and four tranches of bonds denominated in US dollars. The FCY-denominated bonds were issued amid a low-interest-rate environment, with the EUR-denominated issuance diversifying the PRC's holdings of FCY-denominated bonds. These G3 issuances provided benchmarks for Chinese corporations seeking to fundraise in a foreign currency. In November, oil and gas enterprise Sinopec Group issued a triple-tranche, callable, USD-denominated bond with varying tenors and coupon rates to refinance debt and for other general purposes.

The Republic of Korea accounted for an 8.5% share of all G3 currency bonds issued in emerging East Asia during the review period: USD24.4 billion in US dollars, the equivalent of USD3.7 billion in euros, and the equivalent of USD1.2 billion in Japanese yen. Korea Development Bank issued USD1.0 billion worth of USD-denominated bonds in two tranches. Proceeds will be used for general purposes, including the extension of FCY-denominated loans and the repayment of maturing obligations. The Export–Import Bank of Korea issued a USD0.2 billion 5-year bond denominated in euros.

Hong Kong, China accounted for a 9.2% share of the region's G3 currency bond issuance in 2019. By currency, USD30.7 billion was issued in US dollars, while JPY-denominated bonds amounted to USD1.2 billion. Haitong International issued a 6-year USD0.4 billion bond denominated in US dollars, proceeds of which will be used for refinancing debt and other general purposes. Melco Resorts' USD-denominated bond worth USD0.9 billion had a tenor of 10 years and a coupon rate of 5.375%. Proceeds will be used as full repayment of the principal outstanding under Melco Resort's 2015 revolving credit facility and partial prepayment under its 2015 term loan facility.

G3 currency bond issuance among ASEAN member economies increased 3.7% y-o-y to USD60.0 billion in 2019 from USD57.8 billion in the previous year. As a share of emerging East Asia's total, ASEAN's G3 currency bond issuance accounted for 17.3% in 2019, down from 19.7% in 2018, as Indonesia and Singapore experienced decreased issuance. Nevertheless, Indonesia issued the most G3 currency bonds among ASEAN members in 2019, totaling USD22.4 billion, followed by Malaysia and

Singapore, with issuances amounting to USD13.7 billion and USD9.7 billion, respectively.

Indonesia's G3 currency bond issuance in 2019 accounted for 6.5% of the total in emerging East Asia, comprising USD18.0 billion in US dollars, the equivalent of USD2.5 billion in euros, and the equivalent of USD1.9 billion in Japanese yen. The Government of Indonesia issued a 12-year EUR-denominated bond worth USD1.1 billion and with a 1.4% coupon rate. It also issued a 30-year USD-denominated bond worth USD1.0 billion and with a 3.7% coupon rate. The Government of Indonesia took advantage of stable financial market conditions in October via its dual-currency issuance to aid in maintaining the economy's liquidity position. Perusahaan Listrik Negara issued three bonds, two of which were denominated in US dollars and one in euros. Proceeds from the global bonds will be used for capital expenditures to accelerate infrastructure projects and for general corporate purposes.

G3 currency bonds issued in Malaysia accounted for 4.0% of emerging East Asia's total, including USD-denominated bonds worth USD11.4 billion and USD2.3 billion worth of bonds denominated in Japanese yen. Maybank issued four 40-year callable, zero-coupon bonds denominated in US dollars. Sukuk II issued a USD-denominated callable bond worth USD0.2 billion and with a tenor of 5 years and a coupon rate 6.9965%. Proceeds will be used to fund capital expenditure and working capital requirements for its projects.

Singapore's share of G3 currency bond issuance in emerging East Asia was 2.8% in 2019, comprising USD8.3 billion issued in US dollars, USD1.4 billion in euros, and USD0.1 billion in Japanese yen. Totaling USD1.1 billion, Temasek Financial issued two tranches of callable EUR-denominated bonds with tenors of 12 years and 30 years. Proceeds will be used to fund the company's daily operations. DBS Bank issued a 30-year callable, zero-coupon bond denominated in US dollars and worth USD0.1 billion.

The Philippines accounted for a 1.9% share of total G3 currency bonds issued in emerging East Asia during 2019 with bonds denominated in US dollars, Japanese yen, and euros amounting to USD5.1 billion, USD0.8 billion, and USD0.8 billion, respectively. SMC Global and AC Energy issued USD-denominated callable perpetual bonds in Q4 2019. SMC Global's USD0.5 billion bond had a coupon rate of 5.95%, the proceeds of which will be used for the development of battery energy storage system projects and for other general purposes. Meanwhile, AC Energy's green USD0.4 billion bond had a 5.65% coupon rate, proceeds of which will be used for renewable energy expansion across Asia and the Pacific.

During the review period, 1.9% of all G3 currency bonds issued in the region were from Thailand, comprising USD5.9 billion and USD0.6 billion worth of bonds denominated in US dollars and euros, respectively. Kasikornbank issued a USD0.8 billion 12-year callable bond denominated in US dollars. The bonds were issued under the bank's USD2.5 billion medium-term note program. PTTEP Treasury issued a 40-year USD-denominated bond worth USD0.7 billion and with a coupon rate of 3.903%. Proceeds from the issuance will be used to lend to members of the PTTEP Group for liquidity management.

Issuing entirely in US dollars, Viet Nam's share of G3 currency bond issuance in emerging East Asia was 0.3% in 2019, all of which was issued in Q3 2019.

The Lao People's Democratic Republic accounted for the smallest share of G3 currency bond issuance in emerging East Asia at 0.04%, all of which was issued in US dollars.

The proceeds from its issuance of a 2-year USD0.2 billion callable bond with a coupon rate of 6.875% will be used for general budgetary purposes.

Monthly G3 currency issuance trends from January 2018 to December 2019 show a recovery to a monthly average of about USD30.0 billion in the last 4 months of 2019 after a huge drop to USD15.7 billion in August 2019 (**Figure 6**). The uptick in G3 currency issuance in September–December 2019 was spurred by issuances in the PRC, Singapore, and Thailand.

Government Bond Yield Curves

Government bond yields fell for nearly all tenors in all emerging East Asian markets except the Philippines and Viet Nam, where a rise was noted in short-term tenors.

From 31 December 2019 to 29 February 2020, continued moderation in global economic growth led to a downward movement in yields in advanced economies. The potential impact of the spread of the coronavirus disease 2019 (COVID-19) is also weighing on policy makers and financial markets. While some policy makers have said that it is still too early to assess the full economic impact, governments remain vigilant over the possible effects, while rising uncertainty has largely increased risk aversion among investors.

In the US, the Federal Reserve left its policy rate unchanged on 28–29 January 2020, noting that the US economy continues to post gains and the labor market remains resilient. The Federal Reserve also hinted at a slight dovishness, citing concerns that it has been unable to meet its inflation target. Subsequently, the economic outlook for the US worsened following the spread of COVID-19, resulting in an emergency rate cut of 50 bps on 3 March and another 100 bps on 15 March.

In other advanced economies, such as the euro area and Japan, policy makers left their monetary policy stances unchanged at their respective policy meetings on 23 January and 21 January, respectively. Japan, however, did enact a special budget measure in December 2019 to help prop up its economy.

As a result, yields in advanced economies largely fell during the review period. For the US, declining trends were noted for its 2-year and 10-year yields (**Figures 7a, 7b, 8a**, and **8b**). Emerging East Asian economies largely

---

Figure 6: G3 Currency Bond Issuance in Emerging East Asia

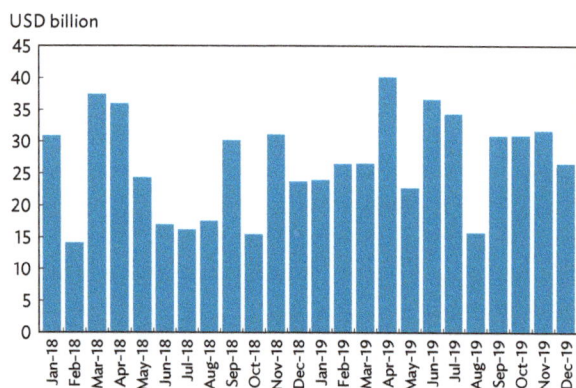

USD billion

USD = United States dollar.
Notes:
1. Emerging East Asia comprises Cambodia; the People's Republic of China; Hong Kong, China; Indonesia; the Republic of Korea; the Lao People's Democratic Republic; Malaysia; the Philippines; Singapore; Thailand; and Viet Nam.
2. G3 currency bonds are bonds denominated in either euros, Japanese yen, or US dollars.
3. Figures were computed based on 31 December 2019 currency exchange rates and do not include currency effects.
Source: *AsianBondsOnline* calculations based on Bloomberg LP data.

Figure 7a: 2-Year Local Currency Government Bond Yields

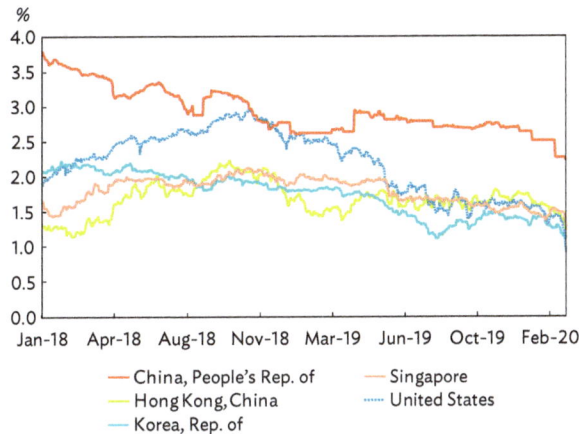

Note: Data as of 29 February 2020.
Source: Based on data from Bloomberg LP.

Figure 7b: 2-Year Local Currency Government Bond Yields

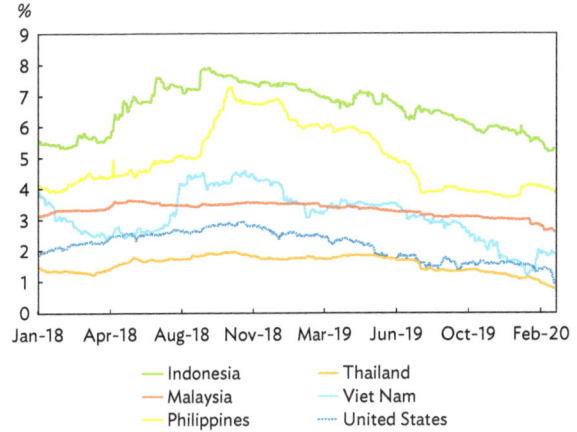

Note: Data as of 29 February 2020.
Source: Based on data from Bloomberg LP.

Figure 8a: 10-Year Local Currency Government Bond Yields

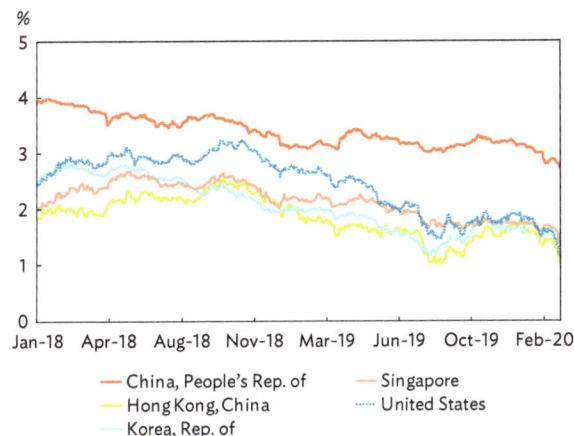

Note: Data as of 29 February 2020.
Source: Based on data from Bloomberg LP.

Figure 8b: 10-Year Local Currency Government Bond Yields

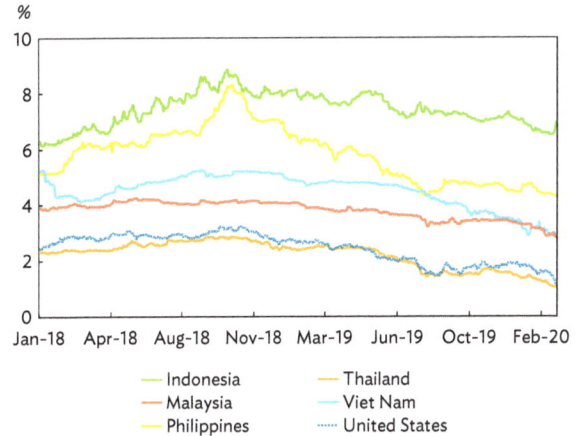

Note: Data as of 29 February 2020.
Source: Based on data from Bloomberg LP.

followed suit. However, a spike in the 2-year yield was noted in the Philippines, Singapore, and Viet Nam before it trended downward for the remainder of the review period.

Emerging East Asia's 10-year yields also generally trended downward. However, a slight spike was noted in the PRC and Hong Kong, China following a boost in investor sentiment after the People's Bank of China (PBOC) intervened in markets to inject liquidity in support of economic growth. The impact of COVID-19, which

originated in the PRC, has weighed on investors and raised concerns over economic growth. The Government of the PRC's efforts to limit the spread of the virus, such as quarantines and the closing of factories, could potentially further slow the economy. Investors are closely eyeing steps being taken by the government to help calm financial markets.

Uncertainty over the potential economic impact of COVID-19 has affected emerging East Asian markets through their linkages with the PRC. While yields were already being pressured downward amid the potential moderation of economic growth, the COVID-19 outbreak has generated greater uncertainty, as evidenced by the downward shift of yield curves in emerging East Asian economies (**Figure 9**). The largest downward shifts in yield curves were seen in the PRC; Hong Kong, China; and Malaysia. The downward shifts in the PRC and Hong Kong, China were largely due to expectations of further weakening in the economy. In the case of the PRC, negative sentiment is being driven by the potential impact of COVID-19, while in Hong Kong, China, the impact of COVID-19 has the potential to further weaken an economy already buffeted by domestic political concerns. In Malaysia, yield declines were largely due to slowing economic growth as economic data released in February showed a weakening economy.

Most yield curves in emerging East Asia shifted downward during the review period, with the two exceptions being the Philippines and Viet Nam. In the Philippines, yield movements were mixed on expectations that inflation would trend upward in 2020. In Viet Nam, yield movements rose at the short-end of the curve largely due to increased funding demand prior to the Tet holiday.

While economic growth has moderated in most of emerging East Asia, inflation has largely been stable. Spikes in inflation were noted in some economies, largely due to either supply shocks or seasonal factors. The most significant rise was seen in Viet Nam where inflation reached a 7-year high of 6.4% in January, driven by the celebration of the Tet holiday (**Figure 10a**).

The PRC also recorded a rise in inflation (**Figure 10b**), exacerbated by both the celebration of the Lunar New Year and supply-side shocks emanating from the spread of COVID-19. Other markets such as the Republic of Korea and the Philippines noted supply-side driven inflation as well.

There were signs of moderating GDP growth throughout the region in Q4 2019. The most significant decline occurred in Malaysia, where Q4 2019 GDP growth fell to 3.6% y-o-y from 4.4% y-o-y in the previous quarter. In Thailand, GDP growth fell to 1.6% y-o-y from 2.6% y-o-y during the same period over delays in the budget's passage. Viet Nam's GDP growth also slowed in Q4 2019, dipping to 7.0% y-o-y from 7.5% y-o-y in the previous quarter. Despite the economic headwinds, the PRC managed to maintain GDP growth of 6.0% y-o-y in Q4 2019, the same rate as in Q3 2019 but lower than in

the first half of 2019. Indonesia also roughly maintained its GDP growth in Q4 2019, posting growth of 4.97% y-o-y versus 5.02% y-o-y in the previous quarter.

The Philippines and Singapore were the only two markets to experience accelerating GDP growth during the review period. In the Philippines, GDP growth climbed to 6.4% y-o-y in Q4 2019 from 6.0% y-o-y in the previous quarter. In Singapore, GDP growth improved to 1.0% y-o-y in Q4 2019 from 0.7% y-o-y in Q3 2019.

While GDP growth somewhat moderated and inflation remained stable in Q4 2019 and early 2020, policy makers in emerging East Asia were confronted by a number of events in January and February that led to increased cautiousness and dovishness. The biggest factor currently weighing on policy makers in the first 2 months of 2020 was the ongoing spread of COVID-19.

Most governments in emerging East Asia that adjusted monetary policy and/or pursued fiscal stimulus cited the potential impact of COVID-19 as a consideration. One exception was Malaysia, where Bank Negara Malaysia was the first central bank in emerging East Asia to cut policy rates in 2020, surprising the market with a 25 bps cut on 22 January to 2.75% (**Figure 11a**). Bank Negara Malaysia said the move was largely preemptive to help sustain the current trajectory of the economy amid potential downside risks.

The Bank of Thailand reduced its policy rate by 25 bps to 1.00% on 5 February, citing a downgraded economic forecast for 2020. While reasons for the downgrade include the budget's delayed passage and adverse weather impacts on agriculture, COVID-19 was also cited. In the Philippines, the BSP reduced policy rates by 25 bps on 6 February, largely due to global uncertainties while also noting that COVID-19 could potentially impact the domestic economy. Bank Indonesia also reduced its policy rate by 25 bps on 20 February, citing it as a preemptive move over the possible effect of COVID-19 on global growth (**Figure 11b**). Following worsening financial conditions and the more rapid spread of COVID-19 globally, central banks in the region became more aggressive. On 3 March, Bank Negara Malaysia cuts its policy rate by another 25 bps this year. The Bank of Korea reduced its base rate by 50 bps on 16 March to 0.75%. Also, the State Bank of Vietnam lowered its refinancing rate by 100 bps to 5.00% effective 17 March. Bank Indonesia and Bangko Sentral ng Pilipinas further reduced their respective policy rates on 19 March.

Figure 9: Benchmark Yield Curves—Local Currency Government Bonds

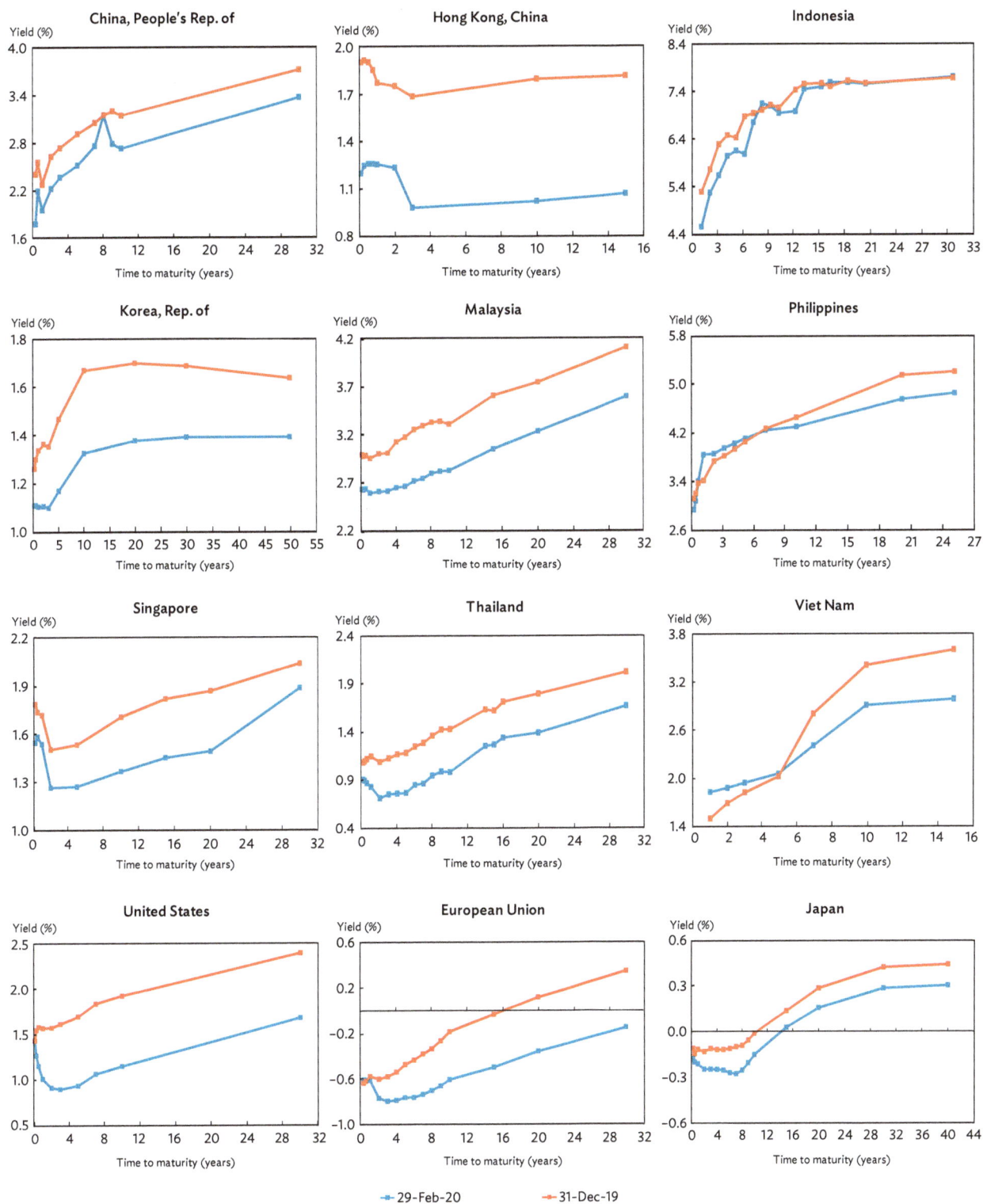

China, People's Rep. of

Hong Kong, China

Indonesia

Korea, Rep. of

Malaysia

Philippines

Singapore

Thailand

Viet Nam

United States

European Union

Japan

29-Feb-20   31-Dec-19

Sources: Based on data from Bloomberg LP and Thai Bond Market Association.

Figure 10a: Headline Inflation Rates

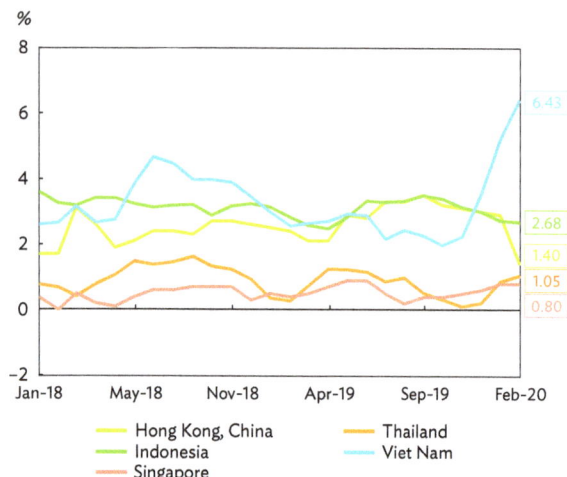

Note: Data as of 31 January 2020.
Source: Based on data from Bloomberg LP.

Figure 10b: Headline Inflation Rates

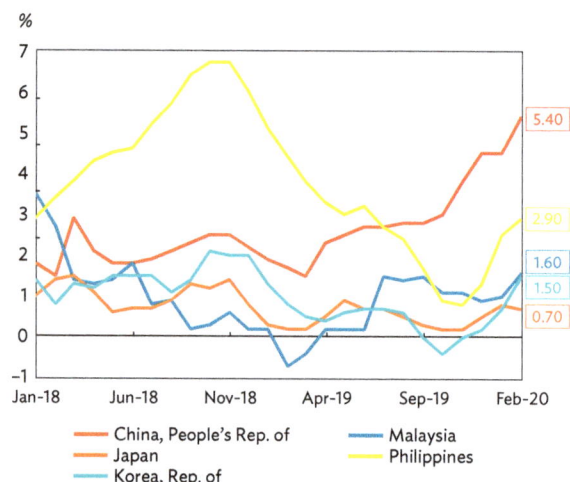

Note: Data as of 31 January 2020.
Source: Based on data from Bloomberg LP.

Figure 11a: Policy Rates

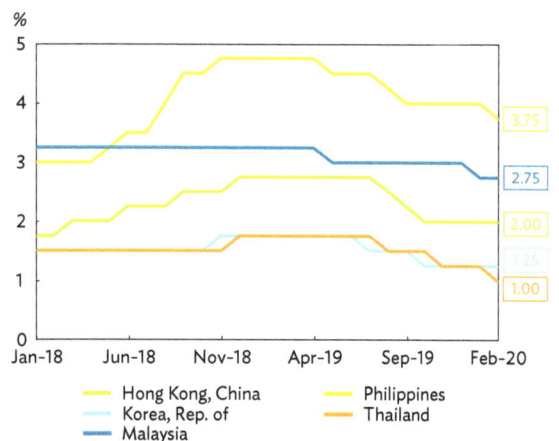

Note: Data as of 29 February 2020.
Source: Based on data from Bloomberg LP.

Figure 11b: Policy Rates

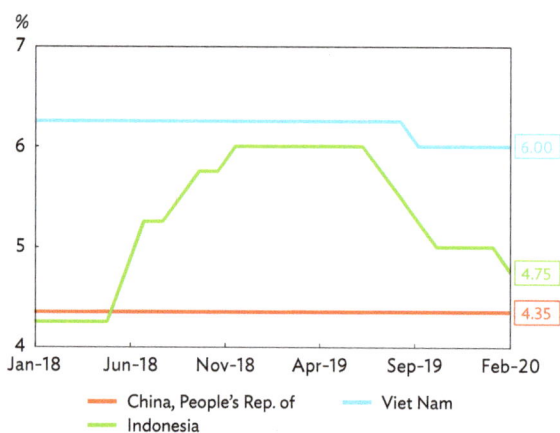

Note: Data as of 29 February 2020.
Source: Based on data from Bloomberg LP.

In the PRC, a number of easing measures have been enacted, due both to an already weakening economy prior to the spread of COVID-19 as well as to curtail the outbreak's negative impact on economic growth. On 31 December 2019, the PBOC reduced the reserve requirement ratios of financial institutions by 50 bps, effective 6 January 2020. On 16 February, the PBOC also reduced the rate on its medium-term lending facility by 10 bps to 3.15%. The PBOC also subsequently reduced the rate on the 1-year loan prime rate by 10 bps to 4.15% and on the 5-year loan prime rate by 5 bps to 4.75%.

In markets that have not engaged in monetary easing, other measures have been enacted to buttress their respective economies. In Singapore, where the MAS's next policy meeting is in April 2020, the government said during its 2020 budget speech that it had downgraded its economic forecast following the COVID-19 outbreak from a range of between 0.5% and 2.5% to between −0.5% and 1.5%. The government also announced a SGD5.6 billion special budget package to prop up the economy. Hong Kong, China likewise announced on 26 February a HKD120 billion package of countercyclical measures to stimulate the economy.

Amid ongoing monetary easing and financial markets bracing for the potential negative effects of the COVID-19 outbreak, the 2-year versus 10-year yield spread fell in all markets in emerging East Asia except Indonesia (**Figure 12**).

The AAA-rated corporate versus government yield fell in the PRC and the Republic of Korea but rose in Malaysia.

In the PRC, the AAA-rated corporate versus government yield spread fell on demand for higher-grade but better-yielding paper, and on hopes that the government would help industries weather ongoing economic challenges (**Figure 13a**). In the Republic of Korea, the spread fell due to an expected recovery in the technology sector. In Malaysia, a rise was noted due to the economic slowdown.

The lower-rated credit spread was largely unchanged in the PRC as investors continued to shun riskier credit (**Figure 13b**). In Malaysia, the spread declined during the review period.

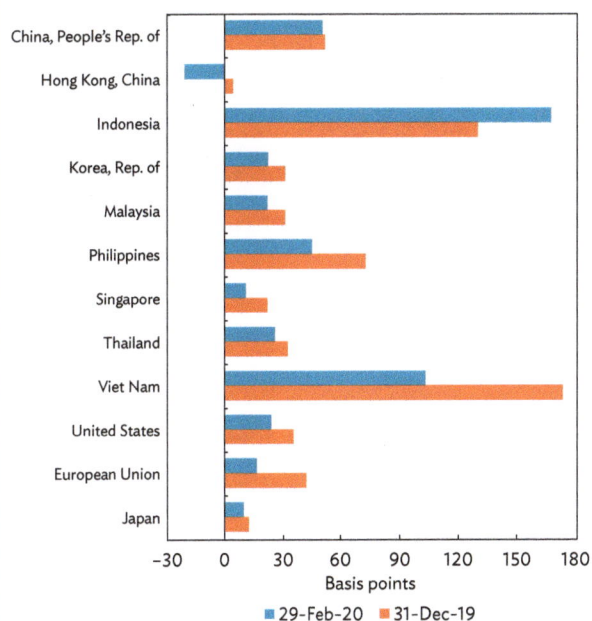

Figure 12: Yield Spreads between 2-Year and 10-Year Government Bonds

Source: Based on data from Bloomberg LP.

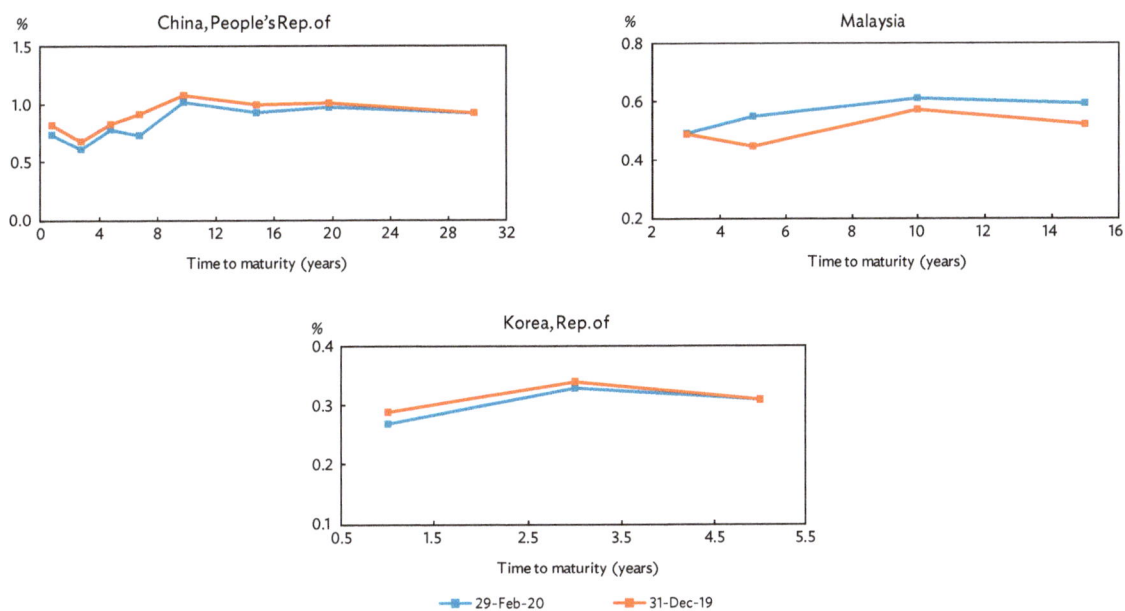

Figure 13a: Credit Spreads—Local Currency Corporates Rated AAA vs. Government Bonds

Note: Credit spreads are obtained by subtracting government yields from corporate indicative yields.
Sources: People's Republic of China (Bloomberg LP), Republic of Korea (*EDAILY BondWeb*), and Malaysia (Bank Negara Malaysia).

Figure 13b: Credit Spreads—Lower-Rated Local Currency Corporates vs. AAA

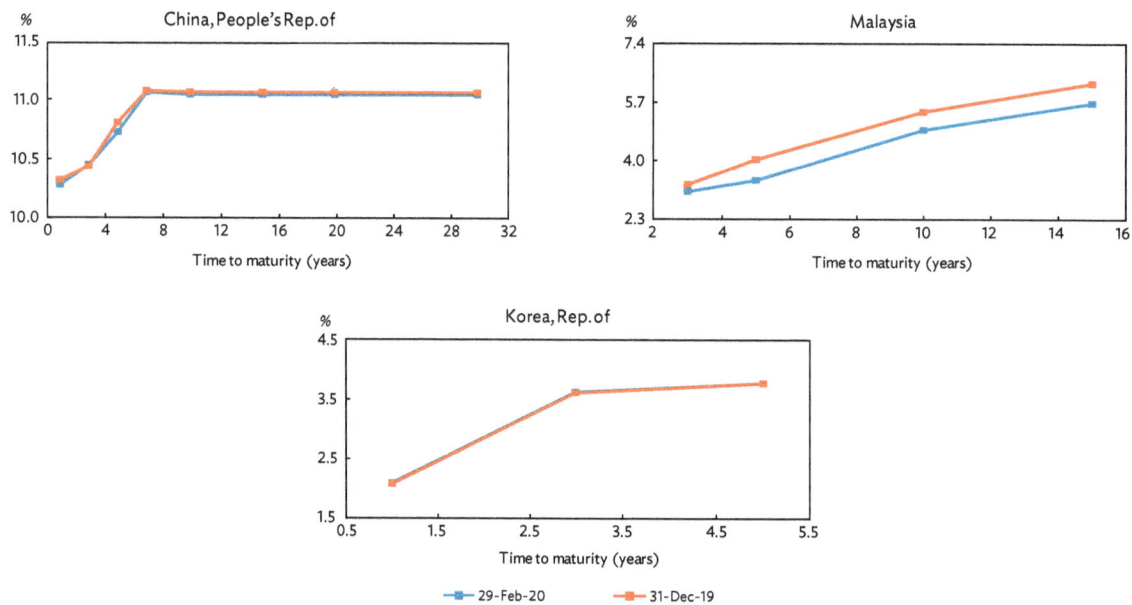

China, People's Rep.of

Malaysia

Korea, Rep.of

■ 29-Feb-20   ■ 31-Dec-19

Note: For the People's Republic of China and the Republic of Korea, credit spreads are obtained by subtracting corporate indicative yields rated AAA from corporate indicative yields rated BBB+.
Sources: People's Republic of China (Bloomberg LP), Republic of Korea (*EDAILY BondWeb*), and Malaysia (Bank Negara Malaysia).

Policy and Regulatory Developments

People's Republic of China

The People's Bank of China Reduces Reserve Requirement Ratio for Financial Institutions

The People's Bank of China (PBOC) announced that it would reduce the reserve requirement ratio for financial institutions by 50 basis points, effective 6 January. The reduction is expected to release more than CNY800 billion worth of funds into the financial system. The PBOC hopes that financial institutions will use the additional liquidity to promote the development of micro- and small-sized enterprises and private companies.

The People's Bank of China Issues Bills in Hong Kong, China

In February, the PBOC issued a total of CNY30 billion of central bank bills in Hong Kong, China, comprising CNY20 billion worth of 2-month bills with a coupon rate of 2.55% and CNY10 billion worth of 1-year bills with a coupon rate of 2.60%.

The People's Bank of China Implements Pilot Program for Treasury Bond Futures for Banks

In March, the PBOC announced that it would implement a pilot program allowing select commercial banks and insurance companies to trade Treasury bond futures at the China Final Futures Exchange. The PBOC's move is meant to help diversify the investor base of the Treasury bond futures market and promote its development. The PBOC also said that the initiative would help banks' risk management and allow them to diversify their range of investment products. Currently, banks and insurance companies are not allowed to trade or invest in Treasury bond futures.

Hong Kong, China

Hong Kong, China Unveils HKD120 Billion Stimulus Package, including Individual Handouts of HKD10,000

At Hong Kong, China's Legislative Council budget meeting on 26 February, the Finance Secretary announced an economic stimulus package worth HKD120.0 billion. The package was designed as a countercyclical measure to bolster the weakened economy, which contracted 1.2% year-on-year in 2019 amid months of political protests. Hong Kong, China's economy is now facing additional challenges brought about by the outbreak of the coronavirus disease 2019 (COVID-19). A cash handout of HKD10,000 for every resident aged 18-years old and above is a key part of the package, which is intended to spur consumer spending and provide financial relief to residents.

The package also features measures to support businesses, including a full government guarantee on loans of up to HKD2.0 million for small and medium-sized enterprises, waivers for certain government fees and charges, reduced rent for short-term tenancies of government land, lower water and sewerage charges, electricity subsidies for transport enterprises, and fee waivers for tourism and securities industries. In addition to the cash handouts, relief measures for individuals include tax rebates, electricity subsidies for households, additional allowances for social security beneficiaries, allowances for students, and waivers for 1 month's rental of public housing. The government had previously rolled out four rounds of relief measures between August and December 2019 worth over HKD25.0 billion.

Indonesia

Bank Indonesia and Japan's Ministry of Finance Sign a Memorandum of Cooperation to Promote the Use of Local Currencies

In December, Bank Indonesia and Japan's Ministry of Finance signed a memorandum of cooperation to promote the use of local currencies for trade and direct investment settlement. The cooperation calls for information sharing and periodic discussion between the two parties. Among other provisions, it provides for exchange rate quotations and interbank trading of the Indonesian rupiah and Japanese yen.

Bank Indonesia Announces Monetary and Financial Stability Measures

In March, Bank Indonesia announced several measures to strengthen monetary and financial stability amid ongoing uncertainties in global financial markets due to the outbreak of COVID-19. Among the measures announced were (i) the optimization of a three-pronged policy to ensure the stability of the Indonesian rupiah through Bank Indonesia's intervention in the domestic nondeliverable forward market, spot market, and government bond market; (ii) a reduction in foreign exchange reserve requirements for commercial banks to 4.0% from 8.0%, effective 16 March 2020; (iii) a 50-basis-points reduction in rupiah reserve requirements for export–import financing, effective 1 April 2020; (iv) an expansion of the range of available hedging instruments for foreign investors; and (v) a reiteration that global and domestic custodian banks may be used by foreign investors for their investment activities.

Republic of Korea

Bank of Korea Lowers 2020 Growth Forecast to 2.1%

On 27 February, the Bank of Korea lowered the 2020 gross domestic product (GDP) growth forecast to 2.1% from a 2.3% projection released in November. A GDP growth forecast of 2.4% was maintained for 2021. The lower GDP growth forecast was due to expectations of weaker consumption in the short-term as a result of the outbreak of COVID-19. Inflation forecasts for 2020 and 2021 were maintained at 1.0% and 1.3%, respectively.

The Republic of Korea Announces COVID-19 Support Package

On 28 February, the Government of the Republic of Korea announced a support package worth more than KRW20 trillion to respond to the COVID-19 outbreak. The package will be partially financed through a supplementary budget. Approximately KRW4 trillion from government reserve funds will be allotted for disease prevention, support for local governments and small businesses, and imports of manufacturing supplies. A total of KRW7 trillion will be allotted for the financial and tax support of families and businesses affected by the outbreak, including a 50% income tax cut for landlords to facilitate rent reduction, along with individual tax cuts for car purchases to boost consumption. The package will also include KRW9 trillion worth of loans, guarantees, and investments to be coursed through financial institutions and public institutions.

National Assembly to Pass KRW11.7 Trillion Supplementary Budget

On 4 March, the Government of the Republic of Korea announced a KRW11.7 trillion supplementary budget to address the COVID-19 outbreak. The supplementary budget will be reviewed and is expected to be approved by the National Assembly. Funding for the supplementary budget will be via KRW10.3 trillion worth of debt issuance and KRW1.4 trillion from surplus funds. Specifically, KRW3.2 trillion is expected to finance expected revenue shortages, and KRW8.5 trillion will be disbursed for expenditures to control and prevent diseases, support small businesses, boost consumption, and support local economies hit by the outbreak.

Malaysia

Bank Negara Malaysia and the Bank of Korea Renew Bilateral Swap Arrangement

In February, Bank Negara Malaysia and the Bank of Korea renewed their local currency bilateral swap arrangement, allowing the two central banks to exchange local currencies with each other up to MYR15.0 billion, or KRW5.0 trillion. The arrangement is valid for a 3-year period, which can be extended by mutual agreement of the two central banks. The bilateral swap arrangement aims to promote bilateral trade and financial cooperation between Malaysia and the Republic of Korea for the development of their respective economies.

Bank Negara Malaysia Issues Guidelines on Domestic Systemically Important Banks

In February, Bank Negara Malaysia issued guidelines on how it will identify Domestic Systemically Important Banks (D-SIBs) in Malaysia. D-SIBs are banks that can potentially cause significant disruption in the domestic financial system and economy if they were to fail. To ensure the stability of the Malaysian financial system, D-SIBs are required to hold higher capital requirements, such as a higher loss absorbency requirement, to mitigate the risk of failure during periods of distress. This requirement takes effect on 31 January 2021. The list of D-SIBs will be updated annually.

Philippines

Bangko Sentral ng Pilipinas Approves Amended Rules on Issuance of Bonds, Commercial Paper, and Long-Term Negotiable Certificates of Time Deposit

In December, the Monetary Board of the Bangko Sentral ng Pilipinas (BSP) approved amendments to rules on the issuance of long-term negotiable certificates of time deposit, bonds, and commercial paper. Related companies of the issuing bank are allowed to underwrite or arrange the issuance of the financial instruments if there are other unrelated third-party underwriters or arrangers. All parties involved must ensure that an objective due diligence review is conducted and that any conflict of interest is avoided. These amendments and reforms aim to promote efficiency in the issuance of the financial instruments and protect the interests of investors.

Bangko Sentral ng Pilipinas Approves Preliminary Policy Initiatives on Islamic Banks and Islamic Banking Units

In January, the Monetary Board of the BSP approved preliminary policy initiatives to advance the implementation of Republic Act No. 11439, which provides the BSP with the legal authority to issue rules and regulations on Islamic banking. These involve policies that will allow Islamic banks to operate alongside conventional banks under the same BSP regulation and supervision, while also taking into consideration the unique features

of Islamic banking operations. Legal provisions would allow conventional domestic or foreign banks to open an Islamic banking unit or a subsidiary Islamic banks, subject to Monetary Board approval. Islamic banks will be required to establish their own Shari'ah Advisory Council to comply with Islamic banking principles.

Singapore

Monetary Authority of Singapore and Bank of Japan Renew Bilateral Swap Arrangement

In November, the Monetary Authority of Singapore and the Bank of Japan renewed their local currency bilateral swap arrangement. The arrangement allows the two banks to exchange local currencies with each other up to SGD15.0 billion, or JPY1.1 trillion, and is valid for a 3-year period. The arrangement aims to provide Japanese yen liquidity to Singapore financial institutions for their intraregional operations.

Thailand

Thailand Rolls Out Additional Fiscal Stimulus to Boost Economy

In October, the Thai cabinet approved an additional stimulus package worth THB5.8 billion to boost the slowing economy. The package included a THB2.0 billion consumption program, the reduction of real estate transfer fees amounting to THB2.6 billion, and low-interest loans from the Government Housing Bank worth THB1.2 billion. This second round of stimulus followed a THB316.0 billion package released in August.

In November, the Government of Thailand rolled out further stimulus to inject THB144.0 billion into the economy to prop up year-end growth. The package included a scheme to strengthen grassroots economies, with THB14.3 billion allotted for villages through the National Village and Community Fund, a THB50.0 billion loan program to support farmers, and a debt moratorium for members of the National Village and Community Fund. A subsidy for rice farmers to support the cost of rice production for the 2019/20 rice crop valued at THB2.6 billion is also part of the package. Another THB5.0 billion was allotted to support home buyers under the Baan Dee Mee Down project.

Thailand Reopens Bond Market to Foreign Issuers

In January, the Ministry of Finance eased its policy restricting foreign issuers of THB-denominated bonds to allow the exchange of proceeds in the foreign exchange market and the remitting of funds offshore. The Public Debt Management Office of the Ministry of Finance noted that there is enough liquidity in Thailand's financial market to remove the restriction that was established in 2016 to stop foreign issuers of THB-denominated bonds from remitting proceeds overseas. The restriction was relaxed slightly in 2017 when the Ministry of Finance allowed exceptions on a case-by-case basis. In 2018, the Ministry of Finance eased the rule further by allowing foreign issuers to exchange a portion of bond sale proceeds to United States dollars as part of efforts to curb the baht's appreciation.

Bank of Thailand Eases Rules to Temper the Baht's Appreciation

In February, the Bank of Thailand eased foreign exchange rules to moderate the baht's appreciation. The central bank increased the threshold of export and income proceeds that do not need to be repatriated from USD0.2 million to USD1.0 million. Exporters with proceeds or income above the new threshold will be allowed to use the funds to offset foreign exchange currency expenses without having to repatriate them. Exporters will only need to register with the Bank of Thailand and provide the necessary documentation.

Viet Nam

Ministry of Finance Announces 13 Market Makers for Government Bonds

In January, the Ministry of Finance announced 13 market makers, comprising banks and securities companies, who will be allowed to participate in the trading of government bonds and government-guaranteed bonds in 2020. The list of market markers includes three securities companies, nine commercial banks, and one member firm of Agribank. As a market maker, these firms may participate in government bond auctions and other issuances of government and government-guaranteed instruments, including debt swaps and repurchase agreements.

Market Summaries

People's Republic of China

Local currency (LCY) bonds outstanding in the People's Republic of China (PRC) grew 2.8% quarter-on-quarter (q-o-q) and 14.1% year-on-year to reach CNY84.2 trillion (USD12.1 trillion) at the end of December. The PRC's bond market growth rate slowed during the fourth quarter (Q4) of 2019, both on a year-on-year and q-o-q basis, compared with the third quarter of 2019. The slowdown in the q-o-q growth was driven by a tepid rise in government bonds outstanding, which grew 2.0% q-o-q in Q4 2019 versus 3.5% q-o-q in the previous quarter.

Table 1: Size and Composition of the Local Currency Bond Market in the People's Republic of China

| | Outstanding Amount (billion) | | | | | | Growth Rates (%) | | | |
| | Q4 2018 | | Q3 2019 | | Q4 2019 | | Q4 2018 | | Q4 2019 | |
	CNY	USD	CNY	USD	CNY	USD	q-o-q	y-o-y	q-o-q	y-o-y
Total	73,770	10,725	81,916	11,459	84,185	12,090	3.4	14.6	2.8	14.1
Government	47,883	6,961	52,913	7,402	53,986	7,753	2.2	14.1	2.0	12.7
Treasury Bonds	14,922	2,169	15,963	2,233	16,698	2,398	3.9	10.3	4.6	11.9
Central Bank Bonds	0	0	14	2	22	3	–	–	57.1	–
Policy Bank Bonds	14,517	2,110	15,445	2,161	15,695	2,254	2.3	7.9	1.6	8.1
Local Government Bonds	18,444	2,681	21,491	3,006	21,571	3,098	0.6	23.0	0.4	17.0
Corporate	25,887	3,763	29,003	4,057	30,199	4,337	5.9	15.7	4.1	16.7
Policy Bank Bonds										
China Development Bank	8,147	1,184	8,665	1,212	8,704	1,250	2.1	8.0	0.5	6.8
Export–Import Bank of China	2,397	348	2,601	364	2,735	393	4.3	4.4	5.2	14.1
Agricultural Devt. Bank of China	3,973	578	4,179	585	4,256	611	1.7	9.8	1.8	7.1

( ) = negative, – = not applicable, CNY = Chinese yuan, LCY = local currency, q-o-q = quarter-on-quarter, Q3 = third quarter, Q4 = fourth quarter, USD = United States dollar, y-o-y = year-on-year.
Notes:
1. Calculated using data from national sources.
2. Treasury bonds include savings bonds and local government bonds.
3. Bloomberg LP end-of-period LCY–USD rate is used.
4. Growth rates are calculated from an LCY base and do not include currency effects.
Sources: Bloomberg LP, ChinaBond, and Wind Information.

Total corporate bond issuance in Q4 2019 reached CNY3.7 trillion, up only 1.7% q-o-q, which was well below the previous quarter's 20.9% q-o-q growth, as market sentiment improved amid a possible slowdown in the United States Federal Reserve's monetary policy tightening. With issuance levels and maturities roughly unchanged from the third quarter of 2019, corporate bonds outstanding grew 4.1% in Q4 2019.

Table 2: Notable Local Currency Corporate Bond Issuance in the Fourth Quarter of 2019

Corporate Issuers	Coupon Rate (%)	Issued Amount (CNY billion)	Corporate Issuers	Coupon Rate (%)	Issued Amount (CNY billion)
China State Railway Group			Bank of China		
3-year bond	3.40	10	2-year bond	3.25	20
3-year bond	3.80	10	10-year bond	4.01	30
5-year bond	3.53	12	Shanghai Pudong Development Bank		
5-year bond	3.50	12	6-year bond	0.20	50
5-year bond	3.60	15	Shaanxi Coal and Chemical Industry		
5-year bond	3.50	12	5-year bond	4.14	3
20-year bond	4.16	8	5-year bond	4.09	3
20-year bond	4.08	8	5-year bond	3.98	5
20-year bond	4.16	8	5-year bond	4.15	4
Bank of Communications			5-year bond	4.15	3
3-year bond	3.35	40			
3-year bond	3.35	50			

CNY = Chinese yuan.
Source: Bloomberg LP.

LCY corporate bonds outstanding among the top 30 corporate bond issuers in the PRC reached CNY9.5 trillion at the end of December, accounting for 31.3% of the total LCY corporate bond stock. The largest issuer remained China Railway, with CNY2.1 trillion of LCY bonds outstanding.

Table 3: Top 30 Issuers of Local Currency Corporate Bonds in the People's Republic of China

	Issuers	Outstanding Amount		State-Owned	Listed Company	Type of Industry
		LCY Bonds (CNY billion)	LCY Bonds (USD billion)			
1.	China Railway	2,138.5	307.1	Yes	No	Transportation
2.	Bank of China	613.8	88.2	Yes	Yes	Banking
3.	Agricultural Bank of China	600.5	86.2	Yes	Yes	Banking
4.	Industrial and Commercial Bank of China	573.2	82.3	Yes	Yes	Banking
5.	China Construction Bank	416.0	59.7	Yes	No	Asset Management
6.	State Grid Corporation of China	413.7	59.4	No	Yes	Banking
7.	China National Petroleum	373.0	53.6	Yes	Yes	Banking
8.	Central Huijin Investment	340.6	48.9	No	Yes	Banking
9.	Bank of Communications	319.0	45.8	Yes	No	Public Utilities
10.	China Minsheng Banking	307.6	44.2	No	Yes	Banking
11.	Shanghai Pudong Development Bank	285.1	40.9	No	Yes	Banking
12.	China CITIC Bank	265.0	38.1	Yes	No	Energy
13.	Industrial Bank	253.3	36.4	No	Yes	Banking
14.	China Everbright Bank	208.5	29.9	Yes	Yes	Banking
15.	State Power Investment	204.4	29.4	Yes	No	Energy
16.	Tianjin Infrastructure Construction and Investment Group	193.6	27.8	Yes	Yes	Banking
17.	Huaxia Bank	189.4	27.2	Yes	No	Industrial
18.	China Merchants Bank	176.7	25.4	No	Yes	Banking
19.	CITIC Securities	173.4	24.9	Yes	No	Banking
20.	Bank of Beijing	155.0	22.3	Yes	Yes	Energy
21.	China Datang Corporation	151.0	21.7	Yes	No	Energy
22.	Datong Coal Mine Group	143.1	20.6	Yes	Yes	Brokerage
23.	Ping An Bank	142.5	20.5	Yes	No	Coal
24.	China Southern Power Grid	136.2	19.6	Yes	No	Energy
25.	China Cinda Asset Management	127.0	18.2	Yes	Yes	Coal
26.	China Merchants Securities	126.5	18.2	No	No	Banking
27.	PetroChina	110.0	15.8	Yes	No	Public Utilities
28.	Dalian Wanda Commercial Properties	108.0	15.5	Yes	Yes	Brokerage
29.	China Three Gorges	107.5	15.4	Yes	Yes	Banking
30.	Shaanxi Coal and Chemical Industry Group	106.5	15.3	Yes	No	Steel
Total Top 30 LCY Corporate Issuers		**9,458.5**	**1,358.4**			
Total LCY Corporate Bonds		**30,199.3**	**4,337.0**			
Top 30 as % of Total LCY Corporate Bonds		**31.3%**	**31.3%**			

CNY = Chinese yuan, LCY = local currency, USD = United States dollar.
Notes:
1. Data as of 31 December 2019.
2. State-owned firms are defined as those in which the government has more than a 50% ownership stake.
Source: *AsianBondsOnline* calculations based on Bloomberg LP data.

Hong Kong, China

The outstanding stock of local currency (LCY) bonds in Hong Kong, China amounted to HKD2,266.0 billion (USD290.8 billion) at the end of the fourth quarter (Q4) of 2019, rising 0.07% quarter-on-quarter (q-o-q) and 1.8% year-on-year. The weak q-o-q growth was largely due to a 0.9% contraction in corporate bonds, which weighed on the 1.0% growth in government bonds. In the government bond segment, the 6.3% q-o-q decline in Exchange Fund Notes nearly offset the 6.9% q-o-q growth in Hong Kong Special Administrative Region bonds and the 0.7% q-o-q rise in Exchange Fund Bills.

Table 1: Size and Composition of the Local Currency Bond Market in Hong Kong, China

| | Outstanding Amount (billion) | | | | | | Growth Rate (%) | | | |
| | Q4 2018 | | Q3 2019 | | Q4 2019 | | Q4 2018 | | Q4 2019 | |
	HKD	USD	HKD	USD	HKD	USD	q-o-q	y-o-y	q-o-q	y-o-y
Total	**2,225**	**284**	**2,264**	**289**	**2,266**	**291**	**2.4**	**16.7**	**0.07**	**1.8**
Government	1,169	149	1,170	149	1,182	152	1.2	1.3	1.0	1.2
Exchange Fund Bills	1,031	132	1,048	134	1,055	135	0.6	2.0	0.7	2.4
Exchange Fund Notes	32	4	28	4	27	3	(5.3)	(14.8)	(6.3)	(17.4)
HKSAR Bonds	106	14	94	12	100	13	9.8	1.0	6.9	(5.4)
Corporate	1,056	135	1,094	140	1,084	139	3.7	40.2	(0.9)	2.6

( ) = negative, HKD = Hong Kong dollar, HKSAR = Hong Kong Special Administrative Region, LCY = local currency, q-o-q = quarter-on-quarter, Q3 = third quarter, Q4 = fourth quarter, USD = United States dollar, y-o-y = year-on-year.
Notes:
1. Calculated using data from national sources.
2. Bloomberg LP end-of-period LCY–USD rates are used.
3. Growth rates are calculated from an LCY base and do not include currency effects.
Source: Hong Kong Monetary Authority.

Among the top nonbank corporate issuers in Q4 2019, New World Development—a diversified company—was the largest issuer with the single issuance of a 30-year bond carrying a 4.89% coupon. Hong Kong Mortgage Corporation was the second-largest issuer, with a dual-tranche issuance amounting to HKD1.2 billion. The quarter saw several other issuances of long-dated bonds. Aside from New World Development, the Hong Kong and China Gas Company and Hong Kong Electric also issued 30-year tenor bonds. The Hong Kong and China Gas Company raised a total of USD0.9 billion from two tranches of 30-year bonds, both carrying a 2.94% coupon, while Hong Kong Electric sold a HKD0.5 billion 30-year bond with a 2.99% coupon.

Table 2: Notable Local Currency Corporate Bond Issuance in the Fourth Quarter of 2019

Corporate Issuers	Coupon Rate (%)	Issued Amount (HKD million)	Corporate Issuers	Coupon Rate (%)	Issued Amount (HKD million)
New World Development			Cathay Pacific		
30-year bond	4.89	1,500	3-year bond	3.38	800
Hong Kong Mortgage Corporation			Hong Kong Land		
0.5-year bond	1.96	770	10-year bond	2.93	550
1-year bond	1.88	400	Wharf Real Estate Investment		
The Hong Kong and China Gas Company			7-year bond	2.46	514
30-year bond	2.94	398	Hong Kong Electric		
30-year bond	2.94	460	30-year bond	2.99	500

HKD = Hong Kong dollar.
Source: Bloomberg LP.

The outstanding bonds of the top 30 nonbank corporate issuers in Hong Kong, China amounted to HKD213.0 billion at the end of Q4 2019, accounting for 19.7% of the total LCY corporate bond market. Government-owned Hong Kong Mortgage Corporation remained the top issuer, with outstanding bonds amounting to HKD28.9 billion. Sun Hung Kai & Co. was the second-largest issuer, with HKD16.7 billion of bonds outstanding. Link Holdings, MTR Corporation, and the Hong Kong and China Gas Company followed, with outstanding bonds of at least HKD12.0 billion each. Of the top 30, only 3 were state-owned. Two-thirds were listed companies on the Hong Kong Stock Exchange. Finance and real estate companies dominated the top 30 list in Q4 2019.

Table 3: Top 30 Nonbank Issuers of Local Currency Corporate Bonds in Hong Kong, China

Issuers	Outstanding Amount		State-Owned	Listed Company	Type of Industry
	LCY Bonds (HKD billion)	LCY Bonds (USD billion)			
1. Hong Kong Mortgage Corporation	28.9	3.7	Yes	No	Finance
2. Sun Hung Kai & Co.	16.7	2.1	No	Yes	Finance
3. Link Holdings	12.2	1.6	No	No	Finance
4. MTR Corporation	12.1	1.6	Yes	Yes	Transportation
5. The Hong Kong and China Gas Company	12.0	1.5	No	Yes	Utilities
6. New World Development	11.7	1.5	No	Yes	Diversified
7. Hong Kong Land	11.0	1.4	No	No	Real Estate
8. Swire Pacific	9.4	1.2	No	Yes	Diversified
9. Henderson Land Development	8.8	1.1	No	No	Real Estate
10. CLP Power Hong Kong Financing	7.7	1.0	No	No	Finance
11. Smart Edge	6.8	0.9	No	No	Finance
12. The Wharf (Holdings)	6.7	0.9	No	Yes	Finance
13. AIA Group Ltd	6.3	0.8	No	Yes	Insurance
14. CK Asset Holdings	6.2	0.8	No	Yes	Real Estate
15. Hongkong Electric	6.0	0.8	No	No	Utilities
16. Swire Properties	5.6	0.7	No	Yes	Diversified
17. Future Days	5.5	0.7	No	No	Transportation
18. Hang Lung Properties	4.6	0.6	No	Yes	Real Estate
19. Hysan Development Company	4.4	0.6	No	Yes	Real Estate
20. IFC Development	3.5	0.4	No	No	Finance
21. Haitong International Securities Group	3.2	0.4	No	Yes	Finance
22. Wharf Real Estate Investment	3.1	0.4	No	Yes	Real Estate
23. Lerthai Group	3.0	0.4	No	Yes	Real Estate
24. Emperor International Holdings	3.0	0.4	No	Yes	Real Estate
25. Guotai Junan Holdings	3.0	0.4	No	Yes	Finance
26. Champion REIT	2.5	0.3	No	Yes	Real Estate
27. China Dynamics Holdings	2.4	0.3	No	Yes	Automotive
28. Urban Renewal Authority	2.3	0.3	Yes	No	Real Estate
29. South Shore Holdings	2.2	0.3	No	Yes	Industrial
30. Emperor Capital Group	2.2	0.3	No	Yes	Finance
Total Top 30 Nonbank LCY Corporate Issuers	213.0	27.3			
Total LCY Corporate Bonds	1,083.8	139.1			
Top 30 as % of Total LCY Corporate Bonds	19.7%	19.7%			

HKD = Hong Kong dollar, LCY = local currency, USD = United States dollar.
Notes:
1. Data as of 31 December 2019.
2. State-owned firms are defined as those in which the government has more than a 50% ownership stake.
Source: AsianBondsOnline calculations based on Bloomberg LP data.

Indonesia

The size of Indonesia's local currency (LCY) bond market expanded to IDR3,310.6 trillion (USD238.8 billion) at the end of December. Overall growth, while positive, moderated to 2.5% quarter-on-quarter (q-o-q) and 16.6% year-on-year (y-o-y) in the fourth quarter (Q4) of 2019 from 5.2% q-o-q and 16.8% y-o-y, respectively, in the previous quarter. The slower growth in outstanding bonds was due to an issuance slowdown in all bond segments in Q4 2019.

Table 1: Size and Composition of the Local Currency Bond Market in Indonesia

| | Outstanding Amount (billion) | | | | | | Growth Rate (%) | | | |
| | Q4 2018 | | Q3 2019 | | Q4 2019 | | Q4 2018 | | Q4 2019 | |
	IDR	USD	IDR	USD	IDR	USD	q-o-q	y-o-y	q-o-q	y-o-y
Total	2,838,177	197	3,229,879	228	3,310,632	239	2.7	13.7	2.5	16.6
Government	2,426,320	169	2,792,335	197	2,865,531	207	3.5	15.0	2.6	18.1
Central Govt. Bonds	2,368,451	165	2,664,332	188	2,752,741	199	2.7	12.8	3.3	16.2
of which: Sukuk	392,985	27	456,844	32	485,534	35	3.9	14.6	6.3	23.6
Central Bank Bills	57,869	4	128,003	9	112,790	8	49.5	477.7	(11.9)	94.9
of which: Sukuk	10,043	0.7	25,674	2	31,174	2	(5.6)	0.3	21.4	210.4
Corporate	411,857	29	437,544	31	445,101	32	(1.7)	6.3	1.7	8.1
of which: Sukuk	21,298	1	30,654	2	30,063	2	25.4	38.4	(1.9)	41.2

( ) = negative, IDR = Indonesian rupiah, LCY = local currency, q-o-q = quarter-on-quarter, Q3 = third quarter, Q4 = fourth quarter, USD = United States dollar, y-o-y = year-on-year.
Notes:
1. Calculated using data from national sources.
2. Bloomberg LP end-of-period LCY–USD rates are used.
3. Growth rates are calculated from an LCY base and do not include currency effects.
4. The total stock of nontradable bonds as of end-December stood at IDR209.3 trillion.
Sources: Bank Indonesia; Directorate General of Budget Financing and Risk Management, Ministry of Finance; Indonesia Stock Exchange; Otoritas Jasa Keuangan; and Bloomberg LP.

In Q4 2019, new issuance of corporate bonds totaled IDR34.2 trillion, down 22.6% q-o-q but up 151.8% y-o-y. A total of 24 firms raised new funds from the debt market during the quarter, adding 68 series of corporate bonds. Among the largest issuers during the quarter were banks and financing companies led by Bank Rakyat Indonesia, Sarana Multi Infrastruktur, and Indonesia Eximbank.

Table 2: Notable Local Currency Corporate Bond Issuance in the Fourth Quarter of 2019

Corporate Issuers	Coupon Rate (%)	Issued Amount (IDR billion)	Corporate Issuers	Coupon Rate (%)	Issued Amount (IDR billion)
Bank Rakyat Indonesia			Perusahaan Listrik Negara		
370-day bond	6.50	738	5-year bond	7.90	796
3-year bond	7.60	2,089	5-year sukuk ijarah	7.90	7
5-year bond	7.85	2,173	7-year bond	8.40	445
Sarana Multi Infrastruktur			7-year sukuk ijarah	8.40	10
370-day bond	6.75	655	10-year bond	8.60	6
3-year bond	7.75	728	10-year sukuk ijarah	8.60	92
5-year bond	7.85	481	15-year bond	9.40	166
7-year bond	8.30	945	15-year sukuk ijarah	9.40	135
Indonesia Eximbank			20-year bond	9.90	500
370-day bond	7.00	600	20-year sukuk ijarah	9.90	554
3-year bond	7.80	101	Kereta Api Indonesia		
3-year bond	7.50	88	5-year bond	7.75	900
5-year bond	8.10	26	7-year bond	8.20	1,100
5-year bond	7.90	1,551			
7-year bond	8.50	112			
7-year bond	8.20	23			
10-year bond	8.75	220			

IDR = Indonesian rupiah.
Note: Sukuk ijarah are Islamic bonds backed by a lease agreement.
Source: Indonesia Stock Exchange.

The 30 largest corporate bond issuers in Indonesia had aggregate bonds outstanding of IDR332.1 trillion, representing a 74.6% share of the corporate bond stock at the end of December. Leading the list were Indonesia Eximbank and Perusahaan Listrik Negara, both of which maintained their respective ranks from the previous quarter. Climbing to the third spot was Bank Rakyat Indonesia, which previously held the fourth spot. All three were state-owned firms that tapped the bond market for funding in Q4 2019.

Table 3: Top 30 Issuers of Local Currency Corporate Bonds in Indonesia

Issuers	Outstanding Amount		State-Owned	Listed Company	Type of Industry
	LCY Bonds (IDR billion)	LCY Bonds (USD billion)			
1. Indonesia Eximbank	37,252.5	2.69	Yes	No	Banking
2. Perusahaan Listrik Negara	29,697.0	2.14	Yes	No	Energy
3. Bank Rakyat Indonesia	25,025.5	1.80	Yes	Yes	Banking
4. Sarana Multi Infrastruktur	22,105.5	1.59	Yes	No	Finance
5. Bank Tabungan Negara	19,847.0	1.43	Yes	Yes	Banking
6. Indosat	16,879.0	1.22	No	Yes	Telecommunications
7. Sarana Multigriya Finansial	14,197.5	1.02	Yes	No	Finance
8. Bank Mandiri	14,000.0	1.01	Yes	Yes	Banking
9. Waskita Karya	13,707.0	0.99	Yes	Yes	Building Construction
10. Bank Pan Indonesia	13,427.0	0.97	No	Yes	Banking
11. Adira Dinamika Multifinance	11,051.2	0.80	No	Yes	Finance
12. Bank CIMB Niaga	9,350.0	0.67	No	Yes	Banking
13. Telekomunikasi Indonesia	8,995.0	0.65	Yes	Yes	Telecommunications
14. Federal International Finance	8,976.5	0.65	No	No	Finance
15. Permodalan Nasional Madani	8,189.0	0.59	Yes	No	Finance
16. Pupuk Indonesia	7,945.0	0.57	Yes	No	Chemical Manufacturing
17. Semen Indonesia	7,078.0	0.51	Yes	Yes	Cement Manufacturing
18. Perum Pegadaian	6,851.0	0.49	Yes	No	Finance
19. Astra Sedaya Finance	6,831.7	0.49	No	No	Finance
20. Hutama Karya	6,825.0	0.49	Yes	No	Nonbuilding Construction
21. Bank Maybank Indonesia	5,831.0	0.42	No	Yes	Banking
22. Medco-Energi Internasional	5,332.2	0.38	No	Yes	Petroleum and Natural Gas
23. Mandiri Tunas Finance	4,730.0	0.34	No	No	Finance
24. Adhi Karya	4,526.5	0.33	Yes	Yes	Building Construction
25. Bank Pembangunan Daerah Jawa Barat Dan Banten	4,500.0	0.32	Yes	Yes	Banking
26. XL Axiata	4,476.0	0.32	No	Yes	Telecommunications
27. Kereta Api	4,000.0	0.29	Yes	No	Transportation
28. BFI Finance Indonesia	3,764.0	0.27	No	Yes	Finance
29. Maybank Indonesia Finance	3,550.0	0.26	No	No	Finance
30. Bank UOB Buana	3,188.0	0.23	No	No	Banking
Total Top 30 LCY Corporate Issuers	**332,128.1**	**23.95**			
Total LCY Corporate Bonds	**445,101.4**	**32.10**			
Top 30 as % of Total LCY Corporate Bonds	**74.6%**	**74.6%**			

IDR = Indonesian rupiah, LCY = local currency, USD = United States dollar.
Notes:
1. Data as of 31 December 2019.
2. State-owned firms are defined as those in which the government has more than a 50% ownership stake.
Source: *AsianBondsOnline* calculations based on Indonesia Stock Exchange data.

Republic of Korea

The Republic of Korea's local currency (LCY) bond market expanded 1.6% quarter-on-quarter (q-o-q) in the fourth quarter (Q4) of 2019 to reach a size of KRW2,407.6 trillion (USD2,083.0 billion) at the end of December. The increase was largely driven by growth in the corporate segment. LCY corporate bonds outstanding rose 2.7% q-o-q to KRW1,455.7 trillion on an issuance surge during the quarter. Meanwhile, outstanding government bonds fell 0.2% q-o-q to KRW951.9 trillion at the end of December due to a decline in the stock of central bank bonds. On a year-on-year basis, the Republic of Korea's LCY bond market expanded 7.6%.

Table 1: Size and Composition of the Local Currency Bond Market in the Republic of Korea

| | Outstanding Amount (billion) | | | | | | Growth Rate (%) | | | |
| | Q4 2018 | | Q3 2019 | | Q4 2019 | | Q4 2018 | | Q4 2019 | |
	KRW	USD	KRW	USD	KRW	USD	q-o-q	y-o-y	q-o-q	y-o-y
Total	2,238,473	2,015	2,370,666	1,982	2,407,623	2,083	0.7	3.8	1.6	7.6
Government	913,966	823	953,854	797	951,912	824	(1.5)	3.5	(0.2)	4.2
Central Government Bonds	567,044	510	607,015	507	611,533	529	(2.1)	3.7	0.7	7.8
Central Bank Bonds	171,640	154	170,960	143	164,060	142	(1.7)	0.5	(4.0)	(4.4)
Others	175,282	158	175,879	147	176,319	153	0.4	6.1	0.3	0.6
Corporate	1,324,507	1,192	1,416,812	1,184	1,455,711	1,259	2.2	4.0	2.7	9.9

( ) = negative, KRW = Korean won, LCY = local currency, q-o-q = quarter-on-quarter, Q3 = third quarter, Q4 = fourth quarter, USD = United States dollar, y-o-y = year-on-year.
Notes:
1. Calculated using data from national sources.
2. Bloomberg LP end-of-period LCY–USD rates are used.
3. Growth rates are calculated from an LCY base and do not include currency effects.
4. "Others" comprise Korea Development Bank bonds, National Housing bonds, and Seoul Metro bonds.
5. Corporate bonds include equity-linked securities and derivatives-linked securities.
Sources: The Bank of Korea and *EDAILY BondWeb*.

Corporate bond issuance in the Republic of Korea surged 30.5% q-o-q in Q4 2019 to KRW157.6 trillion from KRW120.7 trillion in the previous quarter. Table 2 lists some of the notable LCY corporate bond issuances in the Republic of Korea in Q4 2019.

Table 2: Notable Local Currency Corporate Bond Issuance in the Fourth Quarter of 2019

Corporate Issuers	Coupon Rate (%)	Issued Amount (KRW billion)
POSCO Korea		
3-year bond	1.56	610
Shinhan Bank		
2-year bond	1.62	300
5-year bond	1.63	300
Nonghyup Bank		
2-year bond	2.00	340
KT Corporation		
3-year bond	1.55	340
National Agricultural Cooperative		
3-year bond	1.61	340
KEB Hana Bank		
10-year bond	2.42	300

KRW = Korean won.
Source: Based on data from Bloomberg LP.

The aggregate bonds outstanding of the top 30 LCY corporate bond issuers in the Republic of Korea reached KRW899.8 trillion at the end of Q4 2019, comprising 61.8% of total LCY corporate bonds outstanding.

Table 3: Top 30 Issuers of Local Currency Corporate Bonds in the Republic of Korea

	Issuers	Outstanding Amount		State-Owned	Listed on		Type of Industry
		LCY Bonds (KRW billion)	LCY Bonds (USD billion)		KOSPI	KOSDAQ	
1.	Korea Housing Finance Corporation	123,151.9	106.5	Yes	No	No	Housing Finance
2.	Mirae Asset Daewoo	74,883.9	64.8	No	Yes	No	Securities
3.	Korea Investment and Securities	67,042.9	58.0	No	No	No	Securities
4.	Industrial Bank of Korea	59,170.0	51.2	Yes	Yes	No	Banking
5.	KB Securities	54,635.9	47.3	No	No	No	Securities
6.	NH Investment & Securities	51,385.9	44.5	Yes	Yes	No	Securities
7.	Hana Financial Investment	47,488.9	41.1	No	No	No	Securities
8.	Samsung Securities	34,795.7	30.1	No	Yes	No	Securities
9.	Shinhan Bank	31,782.5	27.5	No	No	No	Banking
10.	Korea Electric Power Corporation	28,450.0	24.6	Yes	Yes	No	Electricity, Energy, and Power
11.	Korea Land & Housing Corporation	28,057.7	24.3	Yes	No	No	Real Estate
12.	Korea Expressway	22,810.0	19.7	Yes	No	No	Transport Infrastructure
13.	Woori Bank	20,070.0	17.4	Yes	Yes	No	Banking
14.	Shinyoung Securities	19,648.9	17.0	No	Yes	No	Securities
15.	Korea Rail Network Authority	18,900.0	16.4	Yes	No	No	Transport Infrastructure
16.	KEB Hana Bank	18,320.0	15.8	No	No	No	Banking
17.	Kookmin Bank	16,673.7	14.4	No	No	No	Banking
18.	Shinhan Investment	16,376.0	14.2	No	No	No	Securities
19.	The Export–Import Bank of Korea	16,085.0	13.9	Yes	No	No	Banking
20.	Hanwha Investment and Securities	16,014.0	13.9	No	No	No	Securities
21.	Hyundai Capital Services	15,206.0	13.2	No	No	No	Consumer Finance
22.	Shinhan Card	14,945.0	12.9	No	No	No	Credit Card
23.	NongHyup Bank	14,070.0	12.2	Yes	No	No	Banking
24.	Korea Deposit Insurance Corporation	13,930.0	12.1	Yes	No	No	Insurance
25.	Korea SMEs and Startups Agency	13,847.5	12.0	Yes	No	No	SME Development
26.	KB Kookmin Bank Card	13,310.0	11.5	No	No	No	Consumer Finance
27.	Standard Chartered Bank Korea	12,400.0	10.7	No	No	No	Banking
28.	Meritz Securities	12,328.7	10.7	No	Yes	No	Securities
29.	Korea Gas Corporation	12,098.6	10.5	Yes	Yes	No	Gas Utility
30.	Nonghyup	11,910.0	10.3	Yes	No	No	Banking
	Total Top 30 LCY Corporate Issuers	**899,788.6**	**778.5**				
	Total LCY Corporate Bonds	**1,455,711.0**	**1,259.4**				
	Top 30 as % of Total LCY Corporate Bonds	**61.8%**	**61.8%**				

KOSDAQ = Korean Securities Dealer Automated Quotations, KOSPI = Korea Composite Stock Price Index, KRW = Korean won, LCY = local currency, SME = small and medium-sized enterprise, USD = United States dollar.
Notes:
1. Data as of 31 December 2019.
2. State-owned firms are defined as those in which the government has more than a 50% ownership stake.
Sources: *AsianBondsOnline* calculations based on Bloomberg LP and *EDAILY BondWeb* data.

Malaysia

The local currency (LCY) bond market in Malaysia contracted 0.5% quarter-on-quarter (q-o-q) in the fourth quarter (Q4) of 2019, led by a decline in LCY government bonds, and expanded 6.0% year-on-year to reach MYR1,485.4 billion (USD363.1 billion) at the end of December. LCY government bonds outstanding fell to MYR773.2 billion on a 1.6% q-o-q decrease as central government and central bank bills outstanding contracted in Q4 2019. LCY corporate bonds outstanding amounted to MYR712.2 billion at the end of December on growth of 0.7% q-o-q. A total of MYR937.7 billion worth of *sukuk* (Islamic bonds) was outstanding at the end of 2019.

Table 1: Size and Composition of the Local Currency Bond Market in Malaysia

	Outstanding Amount (billion)						Growth Rate (%)			
	Q4 2018		Q3 2019		Q4 2019		Q4 2018		Q4 2019	
	MYR	USD	MYR	USD	MYR	USD	q-o-q	y-o-y	q-o-q	y-o-y
Total	1,401	339	1,493	357	1,485	363	1.6	8.9	(0.5)	6.0
Government	739	179	786	188	773	189	1.9	9.8	(1.6)	4.7
Central Government Bonds	691	167	749	179	737	180	1.4	8.5	(1.5)	6.7
of which: *sukuk*	306	74	331	79	341	83	1.8	13.7	3.0	11.4
Central Bank Bills	19	5	10	2	9	2	23.9	161.2	(11.8)	(53.1)
of which: *sukuk*	4	0.9	4	0.8	1	0.2	23.3	–	(71.4)	(73.0)
Sukuk Perumahan Kerajaan	28	7	27	6	27	7	0.0	0.0	0.0	(5.6)
Corporate	662	160	707	169	712	174	1.3	8.0	0.7	7.6
of which: *sukuk*	504	122	559	133	569	139	2.2	9.7	1.8	12.7

( ) = negative, – = not applicable, LCY = local currency, MYR = Malaysian ringgit, q-o-q = quarter-on-quarter, Q3 = third quarter, Q4 = fourth quarter, USD = United States dollar, y-o-y = year-on-year.
Notes:
1. Calculated using data from national sources.
2. Bloomberg LP end-of-period LCY–USD rate is used.
3. Growth rates are calculated from an LCY base and do not include currency effects.
4. *Sukuk Perumahan Kerajaan* are Islamic bonds issued by the government to refinance funding for housing loans to government employees and to extend new housing loans.
Sources: Bank Negara Malaysia Fully Automated System for Issuing/Tendering and Bloomberg LP.

LCY corporate bond issuances jumped 2.6% q-o-q to MYR47.3 billion. Danainfra Nasional and Cagamas had the largest issuances in Q4 2019.

Table 2: Notable Local Currency Corporate Bond Issuance in the Fourth Quarter of 2019

Corporate Issuers	Coupon Rate (%)	Issued Amount (MYR billion)
Danainfra Nasional		
7-year Islamic MTN	3.53	0.7
10-year Islamic MTN	3.69	0.4
15-year Islamic MTN	3.93	0.9
20-year Islamic MTN	4.05	0.3
25-year Islamic MTN	4.17	0.3
30-year Islamic MTN	4.29	0.3
Cagamas		
3-year Islamic MTN	3.38	0.3
3-year Islamic MTN	3.38	0.3
3-year Islamic MTN	3.40	0.03
3-year Islamic MTN	3.45	0.1
5-year Islamic MTN	3.55	0.5
5-year Islamic MTN	3.60	0.4

MTN = medium-term note, MYR = Malaysian ringgit.
Source: Bank Negara Malaysia Bond Info Hub.

The outstanding LCY corporate bonds of the top 30 issuers amounted to MYR424.9 billion at the end of December, or 59.7% of total LCY corporate bonds outstanding. Government-owned Danainfra Nasional topped all issuers in 2019. It also led the finance sector to top all sectors with MYR219.7 billion of outstanding bonds, or 51.7% of the aggregate LCY corporate bonds of the top 30 issuers.

Table 3: Top 30 Issuers of Local Currency Corporate Bonds in Malaysia

	Issuers	Outstanding Amount		State-Owned	Listed Company	Type of Industry
		LCY Bonds (MYR billion)	LCY Bonds (USD billion)			
1.	Danainfra Nasional	63.8	15.6	Yes	No	Finance
2.	Cagamas	33.6	8.2	Yes	No	Finance
3.	Prasarana	30.4	7.4	Yes	No	Transport, Storage, and Communications
4.	Project Lebuhraya Usahasama	29.9	7.3	No	No	Transport, Storage, and Communications
5.	Urusharta Jamaah	27.6	6.7	Yes	No	Finance
6.	Lembaga Pembiayaan Perumahan Sektor Awam	22.5	5.5	Yes	No	Property and Real Estate
7.	Perbadanan Tabung Pendidikan Tinggi Nasional	21.6	5.3	Yes	No	Finance
8.	Pengurusan Air	18.0	4.4	Yes	No	Energy, Gas, and Water
9.	CIMB Bank	14.1	3.4	Yes	No	Finance
10.	Maybank Islamic	13.0	3.2	No	Yes	Banking
11.	Khazanah	12.5	3.1	Yes	No	Finance
12.	Maybank	11.6	2.8	No	Yes	Banking
13.	CIMB Group Holdings	11.2	2.7	Yes	No	Finance
14.	Sarawak Energy	11.1	2.7	Yes	No	Energy, Gas, and Water
15.	Danga Capital	10.0	2.4	Yes	No	Finance
16.	Jimah East Power	9.0	2.2	Yes	No	Energy, Gas, and Water
17.	Public Bank	7.9	1.9	No	No	Banking
18.	GENM Capital	7.6	1.9	No	No	Finance
19.	Bank Pembangunan Malaysia	7.2	1.8	Yes	No	Banking
20.	GOVCO Holdings	7.2	1.8	Yes	No	Finance
21.	Tenaga Nasional	7.0	1.7	No	Yes	Energy, Gas, and Water
22.	Bakun Hydro Power Generation	6.3	1.5	No	No	Energy, Gas, and Water
23.	YTL Power International	6.1	1.5	No	Yes	Energy, Gas, and Water
24.	Telekom Malaysia	5.8	1.4	No	Yes	Telecommunications
25.	Rantau Abang Capital	5.5	1.3	Yes	No	Finance
26.	Turus Pesawat	5.3	1.3	Yes	No	Transport, Storage, and Communications
27.	EDRA Energy	5.1	1.2	No	Yes	Energy, Gas, and Water
28.	1Malaysia Development	5.0	1.2	Yes	No	Finance
29.	Jambatan Kedua	4.6	1.1	Yes	No	Transport, Storage, and Communications
30.	Kuala Lumpur Kepong Berhad	4.6	1.1	No	Yes	Energy, Gas, and Water
Total Top 30 LCY Corporate Issuers		**424.9**	**103.9**			
Total LCY Corporate Bonds		**712.2**	**174.1**			
Top 30 as % of Total LCY Corporate Bonds		**59.7%**	**59.7%**			

Notes:
1. Data as of 31 December 2019.
2. State-owned firms are defined as those in which the government has more than a 50% ownership stake.
Source: *AsianBondsOnline* calculations based on Bank Negara Malaysia Fully Automated System for Issuing/Tendering data.

Philippines

The amount of local currency (LCY) bonds outstanding in the Philippine market fell 0.8% quarter-on-quarter (q-o-q) in the fourth quarter (Q4) of 2019 to PHP6,645.8 billion (USD131.2 billion) at the end of December, led by a decline in the outstanding stock of government bonds. LCY government bonds fell 2.1% q-o-q to PHP5,141.1 billion as both Treasury bills and Treasury bonds registered q-o-q declines in Q4 2019. Meanwhile, the Philippine LCY corporate bond market expanded 4.0% q-o-q to PHP1,504.7 billion due to higher issuance during the quarter. On a year-on-year basis, the Philippine LCY bond market grew 9.0%.

Table 1: Size and Composition of the Local Currency Bond Market in the Philippines

| | Outstanding Amount (billion) | | | | | | Growth Rate (%) | | | |
| | Q4 2018 | | Q3 2019 | | Q4 2019 | | Q4 2018 | | Q4 2019 | |
	PHP	USD	PHP	USD	PHP	USD	q-o-q	y-o-y	q-o-q	y-o-y
Total	6,098	116	6,699	129	6,646	131	5.3	11.4	(0.8)	9.0
Government	4,783	91	5,253	101	5,141	101	4.1	7.4	(2.1)	7.5
Treasury Bills	494	9	553	11	486	10	12.6	57.2	(12.1)	(1.6)
Treasury Bonds	4,255	81	4,678	90	4,615	91	3.3	3.8	(1.3)	8.5
Others	34	1	22	0.4	40	1	(0.02)	(16.2)	83.4	18.3
Corporate	1,315	25	1,447	28	1,505	30	9.7	28.9	4.0	14.5

( ) = negative, LCY = local currency, PHP = Philippine peso, q-o-q = quarter-on-quarter, Q3 = third quarter, Q4 = fourth quarter, USD = United States dollar, y-o-y = year-on-year.
Notes:
1. Calculated using data from national sources.
2. Bloomberg end-of-period LCY–USD rates are used.
3. Growth rates are calculated from an LCY base and do not include currency effects.
4. "Others" comprise bonds issued by government agencies, entities, and corporations for which repayment is guaranteed by the Government of the Philippines. This includes bonds issued by Power Sector Assets and Liabilities Management and the National Food Authority, among others.
Sources: Bloomberg LP and Bureau of the Treasury.

Corporate bond issuance in the Philippines surged 42.4% q-o-q to PHP106.4 billion in Q4 2019 from PHP74.7 billion in the previous quarter. Table 2 provides a list of LCY corporate bond issuances in the Philippines in Q4 2019.

Table 2: Notable Local Currency Corporate Bond Issuance in the Fourth Quarter of 2019

Corporate Issuers	Coupon Rate (%)	Issued Amount (PHP billion)	Corporate Issuers	Coupon Rate (%)	Issued Amount (PHP billion)
China Bank			Phoenix Petroleum		
1.5-year bond	5.70	30.00	1-year bond	–	3.50
Metrobank			Ayala Land		
2-year bond	5.50	11.30	5-year bond	4.76	3.00
BDO Unibank			SL Agritech		
5.5-year bond	4.00	6.50	0.25-year bond	–	0.20
Philippine Savings Bank			0.50-year bond	–	0.20
2-year bond	5.60	6.30	1-year bond	–	1.60
Security Bank			Alsons Consolidated		
5.5 year bond	4.00	6.06	0.25-year bond	–	0.20
Robinsons Bank			0.50-year bond	–	0.29
2-year bond	5.13	5.00	1-year bond	–	0.61

PHP = Philippine peso.
Source: Bloomberg LP.

LCY bonds outstanding among the top 30 corporate bonds issuers in the Philippines reached PHP1,327.1 billion at the end of Q4 2019, accounting for 88.2% of total LCY corporate bonds outstanding.

Table 3: Top 30 Issuers of Local Currency Corporate Bonds in the Philippines

	Issuers	Outstanding Amount		State-Owned	Listed Company	Type of Industry
		LCY Bonds (PHP billion)	LCY Bonds (USD billion)			
1.	Metropolitan Bank	128.3	2.5	No	Yes	Banking
2.	Ayala Land	105.0	2.1	No	Yes	Property
3.	SM Prime Holdings	103.7	2.0	No	Yes	Property
4.	BDO Unibank	91.3	1.8	No	Yes	Banking
5.	SMC Global Power	80.0	1.6	No	No	Electricity, Energy, and Power
6.	San Miguel	70.0	1.4	No	Yes	Holding Firms
7.	Philippine National Bank	59.2	1.2	No	Yes	Banking
8.	China Bank	56.2	1.1	No	Yes	Banking
9.	Security Bank	50.8	1.0	No	Yes	Banking
10.	Rizal Commercial Banking Corporation	48.7	1.0	No	Yes	Banking
11.	Vista Land	43.6	0.9	No	Yes	Property
12.	Petron	42.9	0.8	No	Yes	Electricity, Energy, and Power
13.	SM Investments	42.7	0.8	No	Yes	Holding Firms
14.	Ayala Corporation	40.0	0.8	No	Yes	Holding Firms
15.	Bank of the Philippine Islands	37.2	0.7	No	Yes	Banking
16.	Aboitiz Equity Ventures	37.0	0.7	No	Yes	Holding Firms
17.	Maynilad	33.0	0.7	No	No	Water
18.	Aboitiz Power	30.5	0.6	No	Yes	Electricity, Energy, and Power
19.	Union Bank of the Philippines	27.0	0.5	No	Yes	Banking
20.	Manila Electric Company	23.0	0.5	No	Yes	Electricity, Energy, and Power
21.	Filinvest Land	22.0	0.4	No	Yes	Property
22.	San Miguel Brewery	22.0	0.4	No	No	Brewery
23.	East West Banking	21.5	0.4	No	Yes	Banking
24.	Philippine Savings Bank	20.8	0.4	No	Yes	Banking
25.	GT Capital	19.0	0.4	No	Yes	Holding Firms
26.	Robinsons Bank	16.0	0.3	No	No	Banking
27.	Doubledragon	15.0	0.3	No	Yes	Property
28.	PLDT	15.0	0.3	No	Yes	Telecommunications
29.	NLEX Corporation	13.9	0.3	No	No	Transport
30.	Megaworld	12.0	0.2	No	Yes	Property
	Total Top 30 LCY Corporate Issuers	**1,327.1**	**26.2**			
	Total LCY Corporate Bonds	**1,504.7**	**29.7**			
	Top 30 as % of Total LCY Corporate Bonds	**88.2%**	**88.2%**			

LCY = local currency, PHP = Philippine peso, USD = United States dollar.
Notes:
1. Data as of 31 December 2019.
2. State-owned firms are defined as those in which the government has more than a 50% ownership stake.
Source: *AsianBondsOnline* calculations based on Bloomberg LP data.

Singapore

The local currency (LCY) bond market of Singapore expanded 2.6% quarter-on-quarter (q-o-q) and 14.7% year-on-year in the fourth quarter (Q4) of 2019, reaching SGD457.1 billion (USD339.6 billion) at the end of December on the back of increases in both LCY government and corporate bonds. There was a total of SGD285.7 billion in LCY government bonds outstanding at the end of Q4 2019, corresponding to a 3.1% q-o-q increase, mainly due to a rise in Singapore Government Securities bonds. LCY corporate bonds outstanding amounted to SGD171.4 billion at the end of December on growth of 1.7% q-o-q.

Table 1: Size and Composition of the Local Currency Bond Market in Singapore

| | Outstanding Amount (billion) | | | | | | Growth Rate (%) | | | |
| | Q4 2018 | | Q3 2019 | | Q4 2019 | | Q4 2018 | | Q4 2019 | |
	SGD	USD	SGD	USD	SGD	USD	q-o-q	y-o-y	q-o-q	y-o-y
Total	398	292	446	322	457	340	0.1	7.2	2.6	14.7
Government	244	179	277	200	286	212	1.5	10.2	3.1	16.9
SGS Bills and Bonds	125	92	163	118	183	136	2.1	7.7	12.4	46.3
MAS Bills	120	88	114	83	103	77	0.8	12.9	(10.0)	(13.8)
Corporate	154	113	169	122	171	127	(2.1)	2.7	1.7	11.3

( ) = negative, LCY = local currency, MAS = Monetary Authority of Singapore, q-o-q = quarter-on-quarter, Q3 = third quarter, Q4 = fourth quarter, SGD = Singapore dollar, SGS = Singapore Government Securities, USD = United States dollar, y-o-y = year-on-year.
Notes:
1. Government bonds are calculated using data from national sources. Corporate bonds are based on *AsianBondsOnline* estimates.
2. SGS bills and bonds do not include the special issue of SGS held by the Singapore Central Provident Fund.
3. Bloomberg LP end-of-period LCY–USD rates are used.
4. Growth rates are calculated from an LCY base and do not include currency effects.
Sources: Bloomberg LP, Monetary Authority of Singapore, and Singapore Government Securities.

LCY corporate bond issuances dropped 48.9% q-o-q to SGD2.8 billion in Q4 2019. The largest corporate issuance during the quarter came from the Housing & Development Board.

Table 2: Notable Local Currency Corporate Bond Issuance in the Fourth Quarter of 2019

Corporate Issuers	Coupon Rate (%)	Issued Amount (SGD million)
Housing & Development Board		
5-year bond	1.75	700
CapitaLand Treasury		
Perpetual bond	3.65	500
Singapore Press Holdings		
Perpetual bond	4.00	300
Mapletree Commercial Trust		
10-year bond	3.05	250
Hotel Properties		
Perpetual bond	4.40	160
Hongkong Land Treasury		
20-year bond	3.45	150
GSH Corporation		
3-year bond	5.20	50

SGD = Singapore dollar.
Source: Bloomberg LP.

The outstanding LCY corporate bonds of the top 30 issuers amounted to SGD82.7 billion at the end of December, or 48.3% of total LCY corporate bonds outstanding. The government's Housing & Development Board topped all issuers at the end of 2019. It also led the real estate sector to top all sectors with SGD35.3 billion of outstanding bonds at the end of Q4 2019, or 42.7% of the aggregate LCY corporate bonds of the top 30 issuers.

Table 3: Top 30 Issuers of Local Currency Corporate Bonds in Singapore

Issuers	Outstanding Amount		State-Owned	Listed Company	Type of Industry
	LCY Bonds (SGD billion)	LCY Bonds (USD billion)			
1. Housing & Development Board	23.7	17.6	Yes	No	Real Estate
2. Land Transport Authority	10.4	7.7	Yes	No	Transportation
3. Singapore Airlines	4.4	3.3	Yes	Yes	Transportation
4. Frasers Property	4.0	3.0	No	Yes	Real Estate
5. Temasek Financial	3.6	2.7	Yes	No	Finance
6. United Overseas Bank	3.3	2.4	No	Yes	Banking
7. Mapletree Treasury Services	2.7	2.0	No	No	Finance
8. CapitaLand Treasury	2.7	2.0	No	No	Finance
9. DBS Group Holdings	2.5	1.9	No	Yes	Banking
10. Keppel Corporation	2.4	1.8	No	Yes	Diversified
11. Sembcorp Financial Services	2.4	1.7	No	No	Engineering
12. CapitaLand	1.8	1.4	Yes	Yes	Real Estate
13. Oversea-Chinese Banking Corporation	1.5	1.1	No	Yes	Banking
14. City Developments Limited	1.5	1.1	No	Yes	Real Estate
15. CMT MTN	1.4	1.0	No	No	Finance
16. SP Powerassets	1.3	1.0	No	No	Utilities
17. Public Utilities Board	1.3	1.0	Yes	No	Utilities
18. GLL IHT	1.2	0.9	No	No	Real Estate
19. Singtel Group Treasury	1.2	0.9	No	No	Finance
20. Shangri-La Hotel	1.1	0.8	No	Yes	Real Estate
21. Mapletree Commercial Trust	1.1	0.8	No	Yes	Real Estate
22. Suntec REIT	0.9	0.7	No	Yes	Real Estate
23. Hyflux	0.9	0.7	No	Yes	Utilities
24. Ascendas	0.9	0.7	No	Yes	Finance
25. Olam International	0.8	0.6	No	Yes	Consumer Goods
26. SMRT Capital	0.8	0.6	No	No	Transportation
27. DBS Bank	0.8	0.6	No	Yes	Banking
28. Sembcorp Industries	0.8	0.6	No	Yes	Shipbuilding
29. Singapore Technologies Telemedia	0.8	0.6	Yes	No	Utilities
30. National University of Singapore	0.8	0.6	No	No	Education
Total Top 30 LCY Corporate Issuers	**82.7**	**61.5**			
Total LCY Corporate Bonds	**171.4**	**127.3**			
Top 30 as % of Total LCY Corporate Bonds	**48.3%**	**48.3%**			

LCY = local currency, MTN = medium term note, REIT = Real Estate Investment Trust, SGD = Singapore dollar, USD = United States dollar.
Notes:
1. Data as of 31 December 2019.
2. State-owned firms are defined as those in which the government has more than a 50% ownership stake.
Source: *AsianBondsOnline* calculations based on Bloomberg LP data.

Thailand

Total local currency (LCY) bonds outstanding in Thailand rose 2.2% quarter-on-quarter (q-o-q) and 6.4% year-on-year (y-o-y), reaching THB13,236.3 billion (USD445.6 billion) at the end of the fourth quarter (Q4) of 2019. Both the government and corporate segments posted stronger q-o-q growth in Q4 2019 than in the previous quarter. The 2.5% q-o-q growth in government bonds outstanding in Q4 2019 reversed the 1.1% q-o-q decline posted in the previous quarter. All components of the government bond sector posted positive q-o-q growth, with state-owned enterprise bonds and other bonds expanding the most at 4.7% q-o-q. Government bonds comprised 71.4% of total LCY bonds outstanding at the end of December 2019. The expansion of LCY corporate bonds outstanding accelerated to 1.6% q-o-q in Q4 2019 from 0.2% q-o-q in the previous quarter.

Table 1: Size and Composition of the Local Currency Bond Market in Thailand

| | Outstanding Amount (billion) | | | | | | Growth Rate (%) | | | |
| | Q4 2018 | | Q3 2019 | | Q4 2019 | | Q4 2018 | | Q4 2019 | |
	THB	USD	THB	USD	THB	USD	q-o-q	y-o-y	q-o-q	y-o-y
Total	12,445	385	12,946	423	13,236	446	2.5	10.3	2.2	6.4
Government	8,986	278	9,220	301	9,451	318	3.3	9.6	2.5	5.2
Government Bonds and Treasury Bills	4,738	147	4,827	158	4,940	166	2.7	9.3	2.3	4.3
Central Bank Bonds	3,477	108	3,636	119	3,718	125	4.6	14.3	2.3	6.9
State-Owned Enterprise and Other Bonds	771	24	757	25	793	27	1.2	(5.9)	4.7	2.8
Corporate	3,459	107	3,726	122	3,786	127	0.5	12.2	1.6	9.4

( ) = negative, LCY = local currency, q-o-q = quarter-on-quarter, Q3 = third quarter, Q4 = fourth quarter, THB = Thai baht, USD = United States dollar, y-o-y = year-on-year.
Notes:
1. Calculated using data from national sources.
2. Bloomberg end-of-period LCY–USD rates are used.
3. Growth rates are calculated from an LCY base and do not include currency effects.
Source: Bank of Thailand.

Table 2 shows the notable corporate bond issuances in Q4 2019. Global Power Synergy, an energy and utilities firm, was the largest issuer with total issuance amounting to THB35.0 billion from six tranches of bonds with tenors ranging from 3 years to 15 years and carrying coupons ranging from 1.97% to 3.25%. The quarter saw four issuances of perpetual corporate bonds, all with a 5.0% coupon. From their issuances of perpetual bonds, Indorama Ventures, Thai Union Group, Bangchak, and B Grimm Power raised THB15.0 billion, THB6.0 billion, THB10.0 billion, and THB8.0, respectively.

Table 2: Notable Local Currency Corporate Bond Issuance in the Fourth Quarter of 2019

Corporate Issuers	Coupon Rate (%)	Issued Amount (THB billion)	Corporate Issuers	Coupon Rate (%)	Issued Amount (THB billion)
Global Power Synergy			Thai Union Group		
3-year bonds	1.97	2.0	7-year bonds	2.78	2.0
5-year bonds	2.24	5.0	10-year bonds	3.00	4.0
7-year bonds	2.52	6.0	Perpetual bonds	5.00	6.0
10-year bonds	2.86	8.0	Bank of Ayudhya		
12-year bonds	3.15	7.5	2-year bonds	1.72	7.0
15-year bonds	3.25	6.5	3-year bonds	1.80	5.0
True Move H Universal Communications			Siam Cement		
3-year bonds	3.50	6.8	4-year bonds	3.00	10.0
4.25-year bonds	4.10	4.2	Bangchak		
5.5-year bonds	4.70	18.5	Perpetual bonds	5.00	10.0
Indorama Ventures			B Grimm Power		
Perpetual bonds	5.00	15.0	Perpetual bonds	5.00	8.0

THB = Thai baht.
Source: Bloomberg LP.

The aggregate LCY bonds outstanding of the top 30 corporate issuers in Thailand amounted to THB2,135.5 billion at the end of December, comprising 56.4% of the LCY corporate bond market. Food and beverage firms held the largest share of outstanding corporate bonds with an aggregate amount of THB416.9 billion. A majority of the firms among the top 30 were listed on the Stock Exchange of Thailand, while only five were state-owned. Thai Beverage topped the list with THB180.0 billion of LCY corporate bonds outstanding.

Table 3: Top 30 Issuers of Local Currency Corporate Bonds in Thailand

	Issuers	Outstanding Amount		State-Owned	Listed Company	Type of Industry
		LCY Bonds (THB billion)	LCY Bonds (USD billion)			
1.	Thai Beverage	180.0	6.1	No	No	Food and Beverage
2.	Siam Cement	175.0	5.9	Yes	Yes	Construction Materials
3.	CP ALL	152.9	5.1	No	Yes	Commerce
4.	Bank of Ayudhya	136.8	4.6	No	Yes	Banking
5.	True Move H Universal Communication	123.0	4.1	No	No	Communications
6.	Berli Jucker	121.8	4.1	No	Yes	Commerce
7.	Charoen Pokphand Foods	101.0	3.4	No	Yes	Food and Beverage
8.	Toyota Leasing Thailand	86.6	2.9	No	No	Finance and Securities
9.	PTT	84.7	2.9	Yes	Yes	Energy and Utilities
10.	True Corp	82.8	2.8	No	No	Communications
11.	Thai Airways International	74.1	2.5	Yes	Yes	Transportation and Logistics
12.	Minor International	66.0	2.2	No	Yes	Hospitality and Leisure
13.	Indorama Ventures	63.9	2.2	No	Yes	Petrochemicals and Chemicals
14.	CPF Thailand	61.0	2.1	No	No	Food and Beverage
15.	Banpu	48.9	1.6	No	Yes	Energy and Utilities
16.	Krungthai Card	46.2	1.6	Yes	Yes	Banking
17.	Bangkok Commercial Asset Management	45.0	1.5	No	Yes	Finance and Securities
18.	Krung Thai Bank	44.0	1.5	Yes	Yes	Banking
19.	PTT Global Chemical	42.6	1.4	No	Yes	Petrochemicals and Chemicals
20.	Global Power Synergy	40.0	1.3	No	Yes	Energy and Utilities
21.	Land & Houses	39.2	1.3	No	Yes	Property and Construction
22.	Mitr Phol Sugar Corp	38.4	1.3	No	No	Food and Beverage
23.	Bangkok Expressway and Metro	38.2	1.3	No	Yes	Transportation and Logistics
24.	TPI Polene	37.9	1.3	No	Yes	Property and Construction
25.	Thai Union Group	36.6	1.2	No	Yes	Food and Beverage
26.	TMB Bank	35.4	1.2	No	Yes	Finance and Securities
27.	Muangthai Capital	35.3	1.2	No	Yes	Finance and Securities
28.	Total Access Communication	33.0	1.1	No	Yes	Communications
29.	CH Karnchang	32.9	1.1	No	Yes	Property and Construction
30.	Advanced Info Service	32.4	1.1	No	Yes	Communications
	Total Top 30 LCY Corporate Issuers	2,135.5	71.9			
	Total LCY Corporate Bonds	3,785.7	127.4			
	Top 30 as % of Total LCY Corporate Bonds	56.4%	56.4%			

LCY = local currency, THB = Thai baht, USD = United States dollar.
Notes:
1. Data as of 31 December 2019.
2. State-owned firms are defined as those in which the government has more than a 50% ownership stake.
Source: *AsianBondsOnline* calculations based on Bloomberg LP data.

Viet Nam

The size of Viet Nam's local currency (LCY) bond market slipped to VND1,241.1 trillion (USD53.6 billion) at the end of December, down 3.9% quarter-on-quarter (q-o-q) but up 4.1% year-on-year. The q-o-q decline was driven largely by the maturation of all outstanding central bank bills during the fourth quarter (Q4) of 2019.

Table 1: Size and Composition of the Local Currency Bond Market in Viet Nam

| | Outstanding Amount (billion) | | | | | | Growth Rate (%) | | | |
| | Q4 2018 | | Q3 2019 | | Q4 2019 | | Q4 2018 | | Q4 2019 | |
	VND	USD	VND	USD	VND	USD	q-o-q	y-o-y	q-o-q	y-o-y
Total	1,192,004	51	1,291,992	56	1,241,064	54	(4.9)	10.4	(3.9)	4.1
Government	1,082,140	47	1,186,748	51	1,141,009	49	(6.1)	7.9	(3.9)	5.4
Treasury Bonds	898,393	39	955,061	41	978,904	42	0.2	12.8	2.5	9.0
Central Bank Bonds	0	0	71,997	3	0	0	(100.0)	(100.0)	(100.0)	–
State-Owned Enterprise Bonds	183,748	8	159,690	7	162,105	7	1.4	(3.3)	1.5	(11.8)
Corporate	109,863	5	105,244	5	100,055	4	8.8	43.1	(4.9)	(8.9)

( ) = negative, – = not applicable, LCY = local currency, q-o-q = quarter-on-quarter, Q3 = third quarter, Q4 = fourth quarter, USD = United States dollar, VND = Vietnamese dong, y-o-y = year-on-year.
Notes:
1. Bloomberg LP end-of-period LCY–USD rates are used.
2. Growth rates are calculated from an LCY base and do not include currency effects.
Sources: Bloomberg LP and Vietnam Bond Market Association.

New LCY corporate debt issuance totaled VND1.7 trillion in Q4 2019 on declines of 44.8% q-o-q and 86.3% year-on-year. The largest new corporate bond issue during the quarter came from Asia Commercial Joint Stock Bank via a VND1.5 trillion 5-year bond.

Table 2: Local Currency Corporate Bond Issuance in the Fourth Quarter of 2019

Corporate Issuer	Coupon Rate (%)	Issued Amount (VND billion)
Asia Commercial Joint Stock Bank		
5-year bond	7.10	1,500.00
Nui Phao Mining		
3-year bond	10.00	210.00
Vietnam Electric Equipment		
10-year bond	6.95	1.15

VND = Vietnamese dong.
Source: Bloomberg LP.

Viet Nam's 31 largest LCY corporate bond issuers had aggregate bonds outstanding of VND97.7 trillion at the end of December, accounting for a 97.7% share of the corporate bond stock. Vinhomes, a real estate services firm, continued to hold the top post at the end of Q4 2019 with outstanding bonds of VND12.5 trillion.

Table 3: Top 31 Issuers of Local Currency Corporate Bonds in Viet Nam

	Issuers	Outstanding Amount		State–Owned	Listed Company	Type of Industry
		LCY Bonds (THB billion)	LCY Bonds (USD billion)			
1.	Vinhomes	12,500	0.54	No	Yes	Real Estate
2.	Masan Consumer Holdings	11,100	0.48	No	No	Diversified Operations
3.	Asia Commercial Joint Stock Bank	8,300	0.36	No	No	Banking
4.	Vietnam Joint Stock Commercial Bank for Industry and Trade	8,200	0.35	Yes	Yes	Banking
5.	Vingroup	8,100	0.35	No	Yes	Real Estate
6.	Vinpearl	7,500	0.32	No	No	Hotel Operator
7.	Lien Viet Post Joint Stock Commercial Bank	3,100	0.13	No	Yes	Banking
8.	Bank for Investment and Development of Vietnam	3,050	0.13	Yes	Yes	Banking
9.	Hoang Anh Gia Lai	3,000	0.13	No	Yes	Real Estate
10.	Vietnam Technological and Commercial Joint Stock Bank	3,000	0.13	No	No	Banking
11.	Sai Dong Urban Investment and Development	2,600	0.11	No	No	Real Estate
12.	Ho Chi Minh City Infrastructure Investment	2,470	0.11	No	Yes	Infrastructure
13.	Hoan My Medical	2,330	0.10	No	No	Healthcare Services
14.	Refrigeration Electrical	2,318	0.10	No	Yes	Manufacturing
15.	Vietnam International Commercial Bank	2,203	0.10	No	Yes	Agriculture
16.	Agro Nutrition International	2,000	0.09	No	No	Agriculture
17.	Joint Stock Commercial Bank for Foreign Trade of Vietnam	2,000	0.09	Yes	Yes	Banking
18.	Nui Phao Mining	1,710	0.07	No	No	Mining
19.	Masan Group	1,500	0.06	No	Yes	Finance
20.	Masan Resources	1,500	0.06	No	Yes	Mining
21.	Saigon-Hanoi Securities	1,150	0.05	No	Yes	Finance
22.	SSI Securities	1,150	0.05	No	Yes	Finance
23.	Mobile World Investment	1,135	0.05	No	Yes	Manufacturing
24.	Pan Group	1,135	0.05	No	Yes	Consumer Services
25.	TTC Education Joint Stock Company	951	0.04	No	No	Education Services
26.	Sai Gon Thuong Tin Real Estate	870	0.04	No	Yes	Real Estate
27.	Vietnam Bank for Agriculture and Rural Development	760	0.03	Yes	No	Banking
28.	Nam Long Investment	660	0.03	No	Yes	Real Estate
29.	Khang Dien House Trading	534	0.02	No	Yes	Real Estate
30.	An Phat Bioplastics	450	0.02	No	Yes	Manufacturing
31.	Cuu Long Pharmaceutical	450	0.02	No	Yes	Manufacturing
	Total Top 31 LCY Corporate Issuers	97,725.9	4.22			
	Total LCY Corporate Bonds	100,055.0	4.32			
	Top 31 as % of Total LCY Corporate Bonds	97.7%	97.7%			

LCY = local currency, USD = United States dollar, VND = Vietnamese dong.
Notes:
1. Data as of 31 December 2019.
2. State-owned firms are defined as those in which the government has more than a 50% ownership stake.
Source: *AsianBondsOnline* calculations based on Bloomberg LP data.

www.ingramcontent.com/pod-product-compliance
Lightning Source LLC
Chambersburg PA
CBHW051658210326
41518CB00026B/2626